Andrew Ritchie

Heroes and Heroines of the Christian Church

Andrew Ritchie

Heroes and Heroines of the Christian Church

ISBN/EAN: 9783743336957

Manufactured in Europe, USA, Canada, Australia, Japa

Cover: Foto ©Lupo / pixelio.de

Manufactured and distributed by brebook publishing software (www.brebook.com)

Andrew Ritchie

Heroes and Heroines of the Christian Church

Heroes and Heroines

OF THE

CHRISTIAN CHURCH.

BY

REV. A. RITCHIE, Ph. D.

AMERICAN TRACT SOCIETY,
150 NASSAU STREET, NEW YORK.

CONTENTS.

"ST. PATRICK".	7
JOHN WICKLIFFE.	14
WILLIAM TYNDALE	24
JOHN HUSS	34
JEROME OF PRAGUE	46
PATRICK HAMILTON.	55
HUGH LATIMER	61
MARTIN LUTHER.	68
PHILIP MELANCHTHON	83
ULRIC ZWINGLI	97
JOHN CALVIN	114
JOHN KNOX	131
THOMAS CRANMER.	146
JOHN BUNYAN	156
BERNARD PALISSY.	166
HENRY MARTYN.	172
ADONIRAM JUDSON.	182
JOHN NEWTON	195
WILLIAM MILNE	207

CONTENTS.

ROBERT POLLOCK 216
THOMAS CHALMERS 229
JOHN WILLIAMS 242
JOHN COLERIDGE PATTESON 253

ANNE ASKEW 265
LADY MARGARET DOUGLAS . . 270
MRS. ISABELLA GRAHAM 276
ELIZABETH FRY 284
MARY LUNDIE DUNCAN . . 291
HANNAH MORE . . . 298
MARY SOMERVILLE . . 307
ANN HASSELTINE JUDSON 312
SARAH MARTIN 322
LADY HUNTINGDON 330
LADY GLENORCHY 338
MARY LYON 343

EXPLANATORY.

THE sketches in this volume were prepared for and published in "The Christian Press." They were well received, and many requests made for their publication in a more permanent form.

The author has yielded to these requests, believing that the brevity of the sketches and the simple style in which they are written will especially commend them to young readers, and to those who in this busy age want everything in a nutshell. It is here also proper to say that in addition to the volumes mentioned in the sketches themselves, the author is indebted largely for the facts which form the basis of these narratives to "The Life of Lady Huntington," and "The Life of Mary Lyon," published by the American Tract Society, and to the "Five Women of England," and "The Heroes of Bohemia," published by the Presbyterian Board of Publication. The author would be doing violence to his feelings did he not also here acknowledge his great obligation to the editorial corps of the Tract Society, for corrections and revisions preparatory to and during its publication. That the volume may be blessed to the leading of many readers to accept the faith which produced these Heroes and Heroines is our earnest prayer.   A. R.

HEROES AND HEROINES.

"ST. PATRICK."

SOME time in the year 377, while the Roman power was yet in its glory—for Julian and his persecutions had passed away, and Jovian and Gratian had introduced a large degree of liberty, both civil and religious, throughout the empire—there was born in North Britain, in a humble cottage near to a place known as Kilpatrick, a child destined to accomplish a great work in the neighboring kingdom of Ireland, and to have his name pass down in the history of the church as the patron saint of that island. The child's father was named Calphornius; he was the son of the pious presbyter Potitus, who had sent him to France to be instructed in the evangelical religion by the then celebrated Martin of Tours. It appeared afterwards that this teacher had a sister, by name Conche, who had ability to teach the art of loving, and, as a result, she became the wife of Calphornius, and returned with him to his far-off home in Scotland. In due time she became the mother of the hero of our sketch, the celebrated "St. Patrick."

At that period it was no uncommon thing for the Irish Scots to make a raid in Britain, and carry away, along with produce and cattle, such of the inhabitants as they could seize. About the year 393 a band of these marauders passed near the home of Calphornius, and carried away his son, then a lad of some sixteen years. Like Jacob, when Joseph was taken away, his parents no doubt refused to be comforted under such a sad calamity; but, as in Joseph's case, God meant it for good. Though Patrick made his escape to Scotland after a few months, he was again carried off, and for six long years he remained in bondage, almost forgetting his own tongue in the use of the barbarous dialect used among his captors. But he continued free from their superstition and immorality, and longed to bring them to know that religion which was his own solace in sorrow.

In his "Confession"—one of two short epistles which have been preserved from his pen, and which scholars now regard as authentic—he says, "My constant business was *to keep the flocks*. I was frequent in prayers. The love and fear of God more and more inflamed my heart. My faith and spirit were enlarged so that I said a hundred prayers in a day, and nearly as many at night; and in the woods and in the mountains I remained, and before the light I arose to my prayers, in the snow, in the frost, and in the rain, and I experienced no evil at all."

Near the close of the sixth year of these labors, he dreamed that he would find a vessel on the seacoast which would take him back to his parents. He found the vessel, and though refused a passage at first, yet his fervent prayer brought down the Holy Spirit to influence the heart of one of the crew, who took him on board the vessel and protected him. On the third day he reached land, and, after a journey of twenty-eight days, came to his childhood home, where he was received as one from the dead.

The following thirty years of his life cannot certainly be accounted for. It is thought that he visited his uncle Martin, of Tours, and studied, and was ordained to the gospel ministry, and that he then returned, and labored for a short time in his native land. Be this as it may, in the "Confession" to which we have alluded he says, "I saw in my dream a man coming to me from Ireland, whose name was Victorious, with a great number of letters. He gave me one of them, in the beginning of which was the word Hiberniacum. While I was reading this I thought I heard the voice of the inhabitants who lived near the woods of Floclu crying with one voice, 'We entreat the holy youth that you come here and walk among us.' I was greatly touched in my heart, and could read no more; and then I awoke." This determined him to go as a missionary to the land from which, years before, he had escaped.

Mrs. Wright, in her "Early British Church," says: "Tradition is that Patrick, with some companions, landed at Wicklow, and then proceeded to the North, preaching as they went, and making some converts—possibly finding now and then a family holding some remnant of the faith received from Britain. The first object of Patrick was to reach his old master and the scene of his slavery, there to preach gospel freedom. On his way, it is said, he converted a chief named Dicho, who gave him the site of his barn for a church, 'which they carefully built standing north and south, to rebuke superstitions which were rising to assert that the churches must stand east and west.' At Tara, Patrick preached with much success to the king and chiefs; crowds flocked to hear him, and many were converted."

His success continued, and he ordained bishops and presbyters by hundreds and thousands. We suppose, from the numbers ordained, that preachers and elders are meant, and the historic statement of the inspired Word would describe his conduct, as well as that of Paul and Barnabas: "And when they had ordained them elders in every church, and had prayed, with fasting, they commended them to the Lord." Thus, without the authority of pope or bishop, he gave himself to the noble work of preaching the gospel to save the very men who had held him so long in bondage.

There can be no doubt that he accomplished a great work for Ireland. The old legend of his driving all the snakes out of the island had its origin, no doubt, in the driving out of wickedness, and the conversion of wicked men. It is generally believed that he furnished the people with a translation of the Holy Scriptures. The two short compositions to which we have already alluded are said to contain at least forty-three quotations from the Scriptures, and we can easily believe that that which he valued so much, and which in these short epistles he sent to others, he would not withhold from his beloved converts in Ireland.

The first named of these epistles was directed,

in his "Confession," to his "Gallican brethren, and the many thousand spiritual children that God had given him." The other was addressed to Carvdoc, a Welsh chief. They found their way into some of the monasteries, and in those respositories of letters during the dark ages they lay a thousand years, and finally were published about 1660. As a matter of course, the circumstances of Patrick's life gave the Romish priesthood an excellent opportunity to claim that he was one of the Fathers of the Romish Church, instead of being, as he was, a presbyter of the British Church, over which the Bishop of Rome had no authority. It is probable that his labors in Ireland extended through a period of twenty-three years, from 432 to 455, when he died at Armagh, in the seventy-eighth year of his age.

Here it is worthy of note that when Patrick set out on his noble mission, he was about fifty-five years old—an age now-a-days considered almost the age of retirement. The fact that his memory is so revered in the land of his adoption shows the wonderful influence that he must have exerted over the people, and furnished certainly a strong motive to the Roman-catholic Church to claim him as one of her saints, when she had subdued the island and brought it under her control. But long before she was known there he founded a church, and even as late as 1170 the Synod of that old Irish Church, founded by Patrick, met in Armagh, where his bones lay buried, to confess their sins and deprecate the "scourge of God"—the papal soldiers from England now bringing them into subjection to the Romish faith. When this was accomplished, Patrick was claimed as a Romish saint. It is only of late that Protestants have taken the trouble to vindicate his name from this claim, but it has been effectually done by such writers as Archbishop Usher, and Dr. Todd, of Dublin, and our own Mrs. Wright in her work already named.

What a noble act was that performed by Patrick in leaving his home and friends to go to a people who had made him a slave and kept him in bondage six long years, that he might tell the story of the infinite love of God as manifested in the death of his only-begotten and well-beloved Son, to save us. Oh that we had more of the same self-sacrificing missionary spirit in the church of to-day.

JOHN WICKLIFFE.

John Wickliffe was the John the Baptist, or as some one has said, the "morning star" of the Reformation. He was born in 1324, about one hundred and sixty years before Luther, and nearly fifty years before John Huss, in a village in Yorkshire, England, at one of the darkest periods in the history of the church, and as might be inferred, one of the most degraded periods in the history of the country. A writer thus describes the priests of that period: "The main object of those who called themselves ministers of Christ was to enslave the minds and plunder the property of the people committed to their charge; they kept from them the truths of the gospel, and sought to be reverenced as beings superior to their fellow-men, while they indulged every debasing appetite." And with such spiritual leaders, it is easy to believe that the wickedness and profligacy of the people were very great. Subsequently, in one of his tracts, Wickliffe wrote concerning the conduct of parents at this period: "With much travail and cost they get riches and estates and benefices for their children,

JOHN WICKLIFFE

JOHN WICKLIFFE.

and often to their greater damnation; but they incline not to get for their children the goods of grace and a virtuous life."

Wickliffe's parents designed him for the priesthood, and in due time entered him at Queen's College, Oxford, but he afterward connected himself with Merton College. It appears that he made great proficiency in his studies, and—what was strange at that time—he turned his attention to the study of the Scriptures, and, as a result, became dissatisfied with the scholastic divinity of the age.

At about this period the mendicant friars were exerting themselves with much zeal to obtain proselytes among the students, and Wickliffe wrote several tracts exposing their character and designs, one entitled "Of the Property of Christ Against Able Beggary, and of Idleness in Beggary." This opposition at the time gained him popularity, and he was accordingly appointed master of Balliol College and afterward warden of Canterbury Hall, and presented with the living of Fillingham.

At this same period Urban V. demanded the payment of an annual tribute from England of one thousands marks, promised by King John to Pope Innocent III. as an acknowledgment of the pontiff's feudal superiority and right to the disposal of the kingdom. Wickliffe attacked the papal claim. This led him also to examine the character of the Romish prelates, and to publish a treatise on the subject, in which he urges, among other things, "If thou art a priest, and by name a curate, live thou a holy life. Pass other men in holy prayer, holy desire and holy speaking, in counselling and teaching the truth. Ever keep the commandments of God, and let his gospel be ever in thy mouth. Ever despise sin, that men may be drawn therefrom, and that thy deeds may be so far right that no man shall blame them with reason. Let thy open life be thus a true book in which the soldier and layman may learn to serve God and keep his commandments; for the example of a good life, if it be open and continued, striketh rude men much more than open preaching with the word alone." Noble words; but they were not pleasing to Rome. Accordingly the papal court, in 1370, decided against the continuance of Wickliffe in his wardenship. He still, however, continued in the work of preaching the gospel. In 1372 he was admitted as a doctor or lecturer of divinity, and many of his lectures were published, notably one on the Lord's Prayer.

The papal court was in the habit of filling the best offices in the church with foreigners, a

JOHN WICKLIFFE.

thing very detestable to many, even of the strict adherents of the church. Accordingly in 1374 an embassy was sent to the continent to protest against this course of conduct. Wickliffe was one of the delegates, and he returned from Bruges, where the conference with the papal envoys was held, as Luther returned from Rome, with his eyes opened to the enormous wickedness of the pope. He was, he said, Antichrist, "the most cursed of [coin] clippers and purse kervers [cutters]." Wickliffe was soon after appointed a prebendary of the collegiate church of Westbury, and finally rector of Lutterworth.

In the meantime a convocation was called, and Wickliffe was cited to appear in St. Paul's cathedral and answer to the charge of heresy; but the duke of Lancaster accompanied him, and through his influence the trial amounted to nothing. In the same year, 1377, the pope issued a bull addressed to the archbishop of Canterbury, the bishop of London, the king, and the university of Oxford, requiring them to seize and imprison Wickliffe.

He was not seized, but early in 1378 he was cited to appear before his superiors at Lambeth. Edward III. having died, was succeeded by Richard II., and for political reasons the duke of Lancaster now took less interest in Wickliffe's safety. But the people rallied around him, and from this trial also he escaped unharmed. This same year Pope Gregory XI. died, and his death was succeeded by what is known in the history of the church as "the Great Western Schism." For forty years, from 1378 to 1418, two, and sometimes three, rival popes were arrayed against each other, and hurled anathemas at one another, sufficient, one would think, to show that every one of them was Antichrist. This was a favorable period for Wickliffe, and he improved it in preaching and publishing.

It is said that his publications numbered several hundred, and as the art of printing was yet in its infancy and had not come into general use, we can see what labor was involved in the diffusion of these works by the aid of transcribers. Next in importance to the translation of the Scriptures, which noble work we shall notice again, was the volume entitled "Trialogus," consisting of a series of dialogues between three allgorical personages—Aletheia or Truth, Pseudos or Falsehood, and Phronesis or Wisdom. Their discussion embraced the whole round of theology, and of course attacked the errors of Rome, especially caricaturing "Transubstantiation." A convocation of Romish doctors was called soon after the publication of this work, the doctrines of Wickliffe were condemned, and sentence of excommunication was pronounced against all members of the university of Oxford who should teach such tenets.

A synod was called in 1382 by Courteney, the archbishop of Canterbury, who repeated the foregoing sentence. Parliament was then applied to for a law to punish heretics, and the House of Lords passed a bill which, though never really a law, was used as such by the prelates. The statute ran thus: "That divers evil persons went from county to county, and town to town, in certain habits under dissimulation of great holiness, without license of the ordinaries or other authorities, preaching daily not only in the churches and churchyards, but also in the markets, fairs, and other open places where great congregations were assembled, divers sermons containing heresies and notorious errors, etc. It was therefore enacted that all such preachers, and also their favorers, maintainers and abettors, should be arrested and held in strong prison, till they justify themselves according to the law and reason of the holy church before the prelates."

An assembly soon after convened at Oxford, when Wickliffe was cited to answer, and he boldly defended himself and maintained his principles, though with the apostle Paul he could say, "All men forsook me." God however was present with him, and delivered him as far as his life was concerned. But a decree was obtained from the king expelling him and his adherents from the university within seven days.

Wickliffe was at last summoned to Rome to answer before Pope Urban VI., but he excused himself on account of his age and infirmities; and as the rival popes were now engaged in maintaining their claims with carnal weapons, since their anathemas did not end the dispute, Wickliffe escaped.

He continued to labor in his pulpit at Lutterworth and with his pen, for he wrote, "To live and be silent is with me impossible; the guilt of such treason against the Lord of heaven is more to be dreaded than many deaths." He was also engaged at this period in revising his translation of the Bible, from the Latin version called the Vulgate, into English, a work in which he had been assisted by his pupil, Nicholas de Hereford. This was his great work, and it accomplished much for the cause which he advocated. A Romish historian, speaking of it, said, "Wickliffe made a new translation of the Scriptures, multiplied the copies by the aid of transcribers, and by his poor priests recommended it to the perusal of their hearers. In their hands it became an engine of wonderful power. Men were flattered by the appeal to their private judgment; the new doctrines insensibly acquired partisans and protectors in the higher classes, who alone were acquainted with the use of letters; a spirit of inquiry was generated; and the seeds were sown of that religious revolution which in little more than a century astonished and convulsed the nations of Europe."

"By means of colporteurs, then called Lollards, or babblers, a nickname of reproach which the enemies of Wickliffe's doctrines gave to those who professed them, Wickliffe scattered his translation over the kingdom. His devoted followers, with copies of the Psalms, the Gospels or other portions of the Scripture, would start on a tour, and at night would stop at some dwelling, where they were sure of a welcome for the news they would bring. At that period no traveller was ever refused hospitality, for it was through the tales of travellers that those who stayed quietly at home obtained news of the outside world. And our travellers, in detailing their news, would tell of the controversy about religious questions, and recount the arguments of Wickliffe; and after a while, when asked if the Bible really taught such doctrine, the translation would be introduced and sold. Thus the seeds of divine truth were scattered far and wide, and many rejoiced in their new-found Saviour.

But Wickliffe's work was near an end. For two years he had been assisted at Lutterworth by a curate, and yet it is said that he was officiating in the church when seized with the attack of paralysis which ended his earthly life, December 31, 1384. He was peacefully buried in his quiet parish churchyard, but Rome would not allow the remains of such a heretic to rest in peace. Accordingly, the Council of Constance, in 1415, thirty-one years after his death, ordered his bones to be taken up and burned. This order was complied with in 1428, and, as Fuller says, "His dust was cast into the rivulet near by, and carried to the Avon, by the Avon to the Severn, and by the Severn to the sea, and thus his ashes were spread throughout the world, emblematic of the spread of his doctrines."

Concerning this noble man, Milton wrote, "When I recall to mind, after so many dark ages, wherein the huge overshadowing train of error had almost swept all the stars out of the firmament of the church, how the bright and blissful Reformation (by divine power) struck through the black and settled night of ignorance and antichristian tyranny, methinks a sovereign and reviving joy must needs rush into the bosom of him that hears and reads, and the sweet odor of returning gospel imbathe his soul with the fragrancy of heaven. Then was the sacred Bible sought out of the dusty corners where profane falsehoods and neglect had thrown it; the schools were opened; divine and human learning was raked out of the embers of forgotten tongues; the princes and cities came trooping apace to the new-erected banner of salvation; the martyrs, with the unresistible might of weakness, arose, shaking the powers of darkness, and scorning the fiery rage of the old red dragon, and our Wickliffe's preaching was the lamp at which all the succeeding reformers lighted their tapers."

WILLIAM TYNDALE.

In the year 1536 there lay in the prison of Vilvoorden, in the Netherlands, a noted Englishman. A pretended friend, in the pay of the Roman-catholic Church, had, Judas-like, betrayed him to the civil authorities at Antwerp, and now he lies in a prison cell, from which in a short time he will be taken to be strangled, and then his body will be burned. Surely he must have been guilty of some great crime to call for such savage treatment.

What could have been his offence? Nothing, except that he translated the New Testament from the Greek into English, and secured the printing of it, and its circulation among the people. This was the terrible offence which William Tyndale committed, and for which the Romish priests secured his death. But his work still lives, for his translation was the basis of our present authorized version, which is now circulated and read by tens of thousands wherever the English language is known; and even in Rome itself, under the shadow of St. Peter's, the pope is powerless to prevent its use. All honor to the pioneer in this noble work of translating the Bible from the original tongues into English!

William Tyndale was born about 1484, in the Severn Valley, England, and was sent to Oxford to pursue his studies. During his stay there, the edition of the Greek New Testament published by Erasmus in 1516 awakened much discussion in England, as well as on the Continent. Tyndale examined it, and such was the power of its truth on his heart that he was soon suspected of heresy, and, although he had received an appointment as tutor in Cardinal Wolsey's newly formed college, he was obliged to leave Oxford and seek refuge in Cambridge. Here he found two kindred spirits, namely, Bilney and Fryth, who afterwards nobly earned the right to claim the promise, "Be thou faithful unto death, and I will give thee a crown of life," for both, some years before Tyndale, went to heaven from the stake.

Tyndale, however, after a sojourn of two years, found it necessary to leave Cambridge, and happily found a position as tutor in the family of Sir John Walsh, of Sodbury. Having taken orders as a priest, he preached the gospel with such eloquence in a little church belonging to the estate that the people began to think "a second St. John had appeared in bigoted, priest-ridden England." Soon the little church was too small for his audience, and he repaired to a meadow; and multitudes, chiefly from the neighboring city of Bristol, flocked to hear him.

This public proclamation of the gospel produced great excitement among the priests, and soon the preacher's doctrines were attacked. How shall he defend himself? The wife of his patron said to him one day, "Well, there was such a doctor, who may spend a hundred pounds, and another two hundred pounds, and another three hundred pounds, and what were it reason, think you, that we should believe you before them?" Tyndale at once saw the force of her remark, and felt that a standard of doctrine should be provided to which all might appeal; with church authority as the standard, a reformer could make no progress; the Word of God must be placed in the hands of the people as the true touchstone of doctrine. "To the law and to the testimony: if they speak not according to this word, it is because there is no light in them."

Accordingly, Tyndale determined to translate the Scriptures into the vernacular tongue. To use his own words, in speaking of the priests, he says, "A thousand books had they rather to be put forth against their abominable doings and doctrine, than that the Scriptures should come to light. For as long as they may keep that down, they will so darken the right way with the mist of their sophistry, and so tangle them that either rebuke or despise their abominations, with arguments of philosophy, and with worldly similitudes and apparent reasons of natural wisdom, and with wresting the Scriptures to their own purposes, clean contrary to the meaning of the text."

It was now nearly a century and a half since Wickliffe's translation of the Bible was first sent out in manuscript over England. It had circulated extensively for a time, and awakened in many a love for the Scriptures and a disposition to regard them as the only source of religious truth. But the persecution of the Lollards under Henry IV. and Henry V., and their general, though not total, suppression in the reign of the latter monarch, had again shut up the Bible from the English people. And even if Wickliffe's translation had continued to be accessible to English readers, there were reasons why a new version would still have been desirable. First, Wickliffe's translation was wanting in accuracy, being but a translation of a translation—the Latin Vulgate; and, in the second place, the English language throughout this period was undergoing considerable change, so that the language of Wickliffe was very different from the speech in common use in the days of Tyndale. So constant and rapid was this change that William Caxton, the celebrated printer and translator who introduced the printing-press into England in 1476, declared, almost in despair at the mutability of his mother tongue, "Our language now used varieth far from that which was used and spoken when I was born."

Now, though the opposition of the church made every attempt to bring the Scriptures within the reach of the people hazardous, there was still much to favor such an enterprise. The new thirst for learning had revived the knowledge of Hebrew and Greek, the languages in which God gave his Word to his prophets and apostles; and printing-presses were capable of multiplying copies of the Scriptures with speed, accuracy, and comparative cheapness.

In accordance with the Saviour's direction, "When they persecute you in one city, flee ye into another," Tyndale, hoping to find a place in which he might accomplish the work upon which he had determined, now bade farewell to his friends, and turned his steps to London. He had not yet renounced his allegiance to the Romish Church, and so he sought employment as a priest. He was appointed preacher in St. Dunstan's soon after he reached London; and here, as in the little church at Sodbury, his eloquence made him famous, and great crowds flocked to hear him. He soon attracted the notice of Bishop Tonstall, who, if he had not lacked the moral courage, would have befriended him; but, as it was, God raised him up a friend in a merchant named Humphrey Monmouth, who attended his preaching, and gave him a home in his house.

Here he labored diligently at his translation of the New Testament; and after a while he was joined by his friend John Fryth, when the work was prosecuted with increased vigor. But such a work could not escape the argus eyes of priests, and it was soon found that Tyndale must flee to save his life. When informed of the fact, he exclaimed in sorrow of heart, "Alas, is there no place in England where I can translate the Bible!" Then, gathering up his papers, and with ten pounds in his pocket, furnished by his friend Monmouth, he embarked on a vessel bound for Hamburg.

Here he was kindly received by a few Christian friends, and he resumed his work with renewed energy. But having unwittingly received into his employment an unworthy man, he found it necessary to get rid of him; so he left the city and went on a visit to the German reformers at Wittenberg. Thence he repaired to Cologne, with the hope that he might be able to print his

Testament, and have it introduced into England, by means of the facilities which this city offered.

Accordingly, having received some money from his old friend in London, he ordered three thousand copies of his New Testament printed. But one day the printer came to him with trouble on his face: the printing had been interdicted, and he himself was in danger. Tyndale at once fled with his MSS. and finally reached Worms, where, a few years before, Luther had so nobly defended the truth. Here, in the year 1525, some three years later than Luther's German New Testament, Tyndale's English edition was published, and was carried by means of merchant vessels from Antwerp and Rotterdam to England, reaching there early in 1526. Thus this poor priest, hunted from English soil as a wild beast, became one of England's greatest benefactors, and ought yet to have a monument in Westminster Abbey.

Of the reception of Tyndale's translation in England, Taine, in his work on "English Literature," says: "One hid his book in a hollow tree; another learned by heart an Epistle and a Gospel, so as to be able to ponder it to himself even in the presence of his accusers. When sure of his friend he speaks with him in private; and peasant talking to peasant, laborer to laborer, you know what the effect could be. It was the yeomen's sons, as Latimer said, who, more than others, maintained the faith of Christ in England, and it was with the yeomen's sons that Cromwell afterwards reaped his Puritan victories. When such words are whispered through a nation all official voices clamor in vain. The nation has found its *poem;* it stops its ears to the troublesome would-be distractors, and presently sings it out with a full voice and from a full heart."

From Worms Tyndale went to Marburg, to be under the protection of Philip of Hesse, and began his translation of the Old Testament. From this retreat he sent out several editions of the New Testament and other books, including one entitled "The Obedience of a Christian Man," which is said to have been read by Anne Boleyn, and to have disposed her towards Protestantism. In 1529 Tyndale, for some reason, left his safe retreat for Hamburg, with a translation of Genesis and Deuteronomy, which he expected to print there; but the ship was wrecked, and Tyndale lost his MSS. and barely escaped with his life. He afterwards returned to Marburg, and continued there some five years, busy, no doubt, in his work of translating, when he again left Marburg and went to Antwerp.

His enemies in England, who had been a long time seeking to find him, discovered that he was at last within their reach, and a monk was despatched to entrap him and secure his arrest. Accordingly, as we have already stated, he was betrayed by this pretended friend, arrested, and removed to the strong prison at Vilvoorden, a town in Brabant, about twenty miles south of Antwerp. There, on the 6th of October, 1536, he died for the so-called crime of circulating the Bible in the vernacular tongue of the people. It is said that his last words were a prayer for King Henry VIII., who had procured his execution. Even his old adversary, Sir Thomas More, said, when he heard of the result, "Meaner men have worn the bishop's cope."

Yes, few nobler men than Tyndale ever wore a bishop's mitre; few men of any class have done more for Christianity than William Tyndale, and bright must be the crown that he now wears before the throne. Emphatically can it be said of him, "Blessed are the dead who die in the Lord. Yea, saith the Spirit, that they may rest from their labors; and their works do follow them."

Our sketch of this reformer would not be complete without a few more words in regard to the great work for which he laid down his life.

Only parts of his translation of the Old Testament were printed before his death; other parts were left by him in MSS. From Tyndale's versions, and a translation from Latin and German translations, made by Miles Coverdale and published by him in 1535, John Rogers, afterwards the first martyr of Queen Mary's reign, prepared an edition of the Bible, which he, under the assumed name of Thomas Matthew, published in London in 1537, and for which the royal sanction, making it the first authorized version of the Scriptures, was secured. Thus, a year after Tyndale's death, there was circulated by the license of the king a work in which was incorporated the same translation which this same king had repeatedly condemned, and had actually prohibited seven years before. What a triumph for the friends of Tyndale and for all the lovers of the truth! Now "England," as Taine says, "had her book. Every one... who could buy this book either read it assiduously or had it read to him by others, and many well advanced in years learned to read with the same object."

A revision of the "Thomas Matthew" edition appeared in 1539, and was known, from its large size, as the Great Bible. This, again, was revised about 1563, the new revision being called the Bishops' Bible, from the circumstance that eight bishops were among the revisers. And, finally, upon the Bishops' Bible our own King James' Version of 1611 was based.

JOHN HUSS.

OUTSIDE the gate of Constance, a free city in the Grand Duchy of Baden, Germany, on July 6, in the year 1415, there stood, surrounded by a large crowd of all classes and conditions of people, a man fastened to the stake by a chain, while around him were the fagots which would soon consume his body. Looking around on the multitude, this man said, "The chief aim of all my declarations, teachings, and writings has been to bring men to repentance and the forgiveness of sins, according to the truths of the gospel of Christ and the teachings of the Fathers. I gladly this day seal that truth which I have written and proclaimed with the pledge of my death."

John Huss, who made this noble declaration, had just been condemned by the Council of Constance. He had come from his native Bohemia trusting in a promise that a safe-conduct, or guaranty of personal safety, would be furnished him by the emperor of Germany, and soon after his arrival at Constance the safe-conduct had actually been presented to him. But the dignitaries of the Catholic Church, acting on the principle "that faith is not to be kept with heretics," disregarded the imperial assurance, arrested Huss, gave him the form of a trial, and condemned him to be burned at the stake, because it was shown that he favored in some measure the doctrines of Wickliffe. His life, however, was not ended until he had accomplished a great work for the cause of the Redeemer, and doubtless his death added much to the effect of the doctrine he had so ably proclaimed.

Huss was born July 6, 1369, in Bohemia, in the village of Hussinetz, whence he derived his surname, abbreviated by himself from Hussinetz, or de Hussinetz. At this time Charles IV., emperor of Germany, resided at Prague, in Bohemia, and his daughter Anne was afterwards married to King Richard II. of England. This connection became the means of opening up intercourse between the two kingdoms, and aided largely in introducing the doctrines of Wickliffe into Bohemia. The first university established in the German Empire was founded at Prague by Charles IV., in 1348, some twenty-one years before the birth of our reformer. This institution, which soon became the rival of the already famous universities of Oxford, Paris, and Bologne, exerted a strong influence throughout the empire in favor of independent investigation, and thus prepared the people for listening to the doctrine of such men as Huss. The first school to which John was sent was a monastery, where his extraordinary progress attracted the attention of his teachers; and when his father died and left his family in poverty, a noble of the village took charge of the bright boy's education, and sent him to a High School, where he graduated. But the desire for greater educational advantages was burning in his bosom, and he determined to go to Prague. God had work for him to do, and implanted this desire in his heart that he might seek the necessary preparation for it. Accordingly, he told his mother that God would take care of them, and she accompanied him to Prague, where he entered the university in 1389. Here he found able professors and crowds of students, many of them men whose hearts God had touched, and who sought to know the truth, and accepted it, fearless of the results that might come to them from advocating it. Indeed, it would seem as if Huss was impressed with the thought, at this early period of his history, that he would be called to suffer. Accordingly, it is said that he once thrust his hand into the fire to test his power of endurance, as if to embolden himself for his coming fate.

At this period the forty years' schism of the

papacy, which arrayed a French pope against an Italian pope, unsettling the minds even of those who were disposed to be obedient children of the pontiff, was raging in all its fury. When one pope hurled his anathemas at the other, and the other replied, calling his opposer a heretic, a thief, a despot, a traitor, it was natural to conclude that neither of them was the infallible head of the church, as both claimed to be; and thus many people were prepared to listen to what the Bible had to say respecting the question.

Huss received the degrees of Bachelor of Arts, Bachelor of Theology, and Master of Arts, in 1393, 1394, and 1396 respectively; and such was his reputation as a scholar that in 1401 he was elected Dean of the Philosophical Faculty, and afterwards was selected as confessor to the queen of Bohemia. These positions secured for him many friends, and an opportunity to proclaim the truths of the gospel. His career, however, as a preacher, did not fully begin until 1402, when he was made pastor of Bethlehem chapel, Prague— a building reared by private munificence for the purpose of preaching the Word of God in the language of the people; for the services of the churches, being almost wholly in the Latin tongue, could not be understood by the common people. The chapel was chiefly erected and probably sustained by the beneficence of John of Mulheim, a man zealous for the spread of gospel truth; to Huss it was the throne of his power, where he was enabled to expose with trumpet-tongue the ignorance, drunkenness, and avarice of the popish priesthood.

In 1405 Archbishop Sbynko, of Prague, appointed Huss one of the three commissioners to examine into an alleged miracle whose fame was drawing crowds of pilgrims to Wilsnack, near Wittenberg. On the unfavorable report of the commissioners, the archbishop forbade pilgrimages to Wilsnack from Bohemia, and sanctioned the publication of a treatise by Huss condemning pretended miracles and ecclesiastical greed, and urging Christians to look for Christ's presence in his Word rather than in sensible signs.

In the meantime, Huss was making great progress in reformation principles, for, like Luther, the prejudices of his mind were all in favor of the Romish Church; so that when his friend and fellow-martyr, Jerome, showed him, on his return from Oxford, one of Wickliffe's theological books, he advised him to burn it or throw it into the river Moldau. But after a while, when one of Huss' associates saw him reading one of the books of this arch-heretic, and reminded him of the condemnation of his doctrines, Huss replied,

"I only wish that my soul, when it leaves the body, may reach the place where the soul of this excellent writer dwells." He afterwards translated and circulated Wickliffe's books, and recommended them from his pulpit.

Archbishop Sbynko continued for several years friendly to Huss, whom he had invited to assist him in introducing a stricter discipline into his diocese; but Huss entered more warmly into the cause of reform than the archbishop desired, and this circumstance, together with other occurrences, finally led to a disagreement between them.

In 1409 Pope Alexander V., influenced probably by Sbynko, issued a bull condemning Wickliffe's writings, requiring the abjuration of his doctrines, and prohibiting preaching anywhere except in the regular churches. In obedience to this bull, two hundred volumes of Wickliffe's works were committed to the flames in Prague, and Huss was prohibited from preaching in Bethlehem Chapel.

But Huss felt, like Paul, "Woe is me if I preach not the gospel;" he appealed to the pope, and continued to preach. The people and court of Bohemia stood by him, but there was no hope of success at Rome, and finally Huss was summoned to appear at Bologna, and defend himself before the pope. By the advice of friends he refused to undertake such a journey, and was excommunicated in March, 1411; and when he refused to pay any attention to this, Prague was placed under interdict. In that period of spiritual darkness, this was one of Rome's most powerful weapons. It prohibited public religious services of every kind, and even the Christian burial of the dead. This edict, however, brought the king to the defence of Huss, and the archbishop was compelled to beg the pope to annul the sentence against him. The pope did so, and appointed a commission in the case, who revoked the interdict, which, however, had not been observed. Previous to this, in 1410, Pope Alexander V. had died, and had been succeeded by John XXIII., one of the vilest characters of history. With him the controversy went on, being aggravated by Huss' vigorous opposition to the offer of an indulgence, or remission of past and future sins, proclaimed in Bohemia by papal envoys to all who should assist in a crusade against the excommunicated King Ladislaus of Naples. At last the pope renewed Huss' sentence of excommunication, and ordered that his person should be seized and delivered up to the archbishop of Prague to be burned, that every place that harbored him should be laid under interdict, and that Bethlehem Chapel should be torn down. The adherents of Huss were determined, however, to protect him and the chapel from violence; and the king, though he allowed the publication of the bull, would do nothing to execute it; so Huss continued to preach to crowds in his chapel, while the parish priests from their pulpits proclaimed him excommunicated, and strictly observed the interdict under which the city lay for sheltering the rebel against the pope. So serious were the disturbances that ensued that finally King Wenceslaus himself requested Huss to leave Prague, in order that peace might be restored to it.

About this time the reformer published a treatise in Latin, in which he took the ground that "Christ, and not man, is the supreme Head of the church. . . . . The pope is not the successor of Christ or Peter merely by virtue of his office, but only as he resembles them in spirit, in faith, humility, and love," etc. "The office of pope is not necessary to the church; only deacons and presbyters are named as officers in the church in the Scriptures," etc. "Not every priest is a saint, but every saint is a priest," etc. During his absence from Prague he occasionally wrote to his beloved flock such words as these: "Pray for me, that I may more richly write and preach against Antichrist, and that God may lead me in the battle, and when I am driven to the greatest straits in defence of his truth. For know that I shrink not from giving up this poor body for God's truth to those who need it." The very persecution which drove him into exile was the means of sending the gospel to thousands who otherwise would not have heard it; for from his retreats in the castles of noble friends he went forth and preached to crowds who gathered to hear him.

The unsettled state of the church, which the late Council of Pisa (1409) had failed to unite—no less than three popes, John XXIII., Gregory XII., and Benedict XIII., now claiming supreme authority—demanded another general council; and this John XXIII., who had fled to the Emperor Sigismund for protection, was prevailed upon to appoint to be held at Constance, in November, 1414. Pope John himself, though contrary to his purpose, attended it; and thirty cardinals, one hundred and fifty bishops, eighteen hundred priests, the emperor, and numerous princes, noblemen, and knights were present. As the troubles in Bohemia were recognized to be of so serious a nature as to require the immediate attention of the council, the emperor summoned Huss to appear, and promised him a safe-conduct, securing his return to Bohemia. Notwithstanding this, however, many of his friends were alarmed, and expressed their fear that he would never return. But, animated by the same spirit that led Luther to Worms, he undertook the journey, and was warmly welcomed by many friends of reform in the different cities through which he passed.

Four weeks after his arrival at Constance, and before he had obtained a hearing, he was imprisoned by order of the cardinals; and when his friends besought the emperor on his behalf, Sigismund, though expressing indignation at the treatment of Huss, declined to interfere, influenced by the apprehension that his espousal of the prisoner's cause might lead to the dissolution of the council before it had accomplished the purposes for which it had convened. Meantime, confinement and bad air proved injurious to Huss' health, and his enemies feared at times that a natural death would rob them of their victim.

After the flight of John XXIII., to avoid fulfilling his promise to renounce the papal dignity, Huss' condition became still worse; for, after suffering from hunger for some days, his attendants having fled with their master the pope, he was removed, March 25, 1415, from the Dominican convent cell to the castle of Gottleben. Here, under the surveillance of the bishop of Constance, his keepers were harsh, and his friends were forbidden to visit him; he was kept in chains during the day, and at night was fastened to a post. Still, however, like Paul in his Roman dungeon, he was sustained by the comforts of Christ, and, by his conduct and in letters that he wrote, expressed cheerful submission to the will of God.

At length, through the exertions of his friends, he was brought before the council on the 5th of June; but he was received with such outcries of "Recant," etc., that he found it impossible to defend himself. Indeed, the verdict of guilty had already been determined on by his judges; justice and fair dealing could not be obtained. At length the council adjourned until June 7th, and then and on the following day Huss, in his chains, was again brought before the council, while extracts, declared to be heretical, were read from his writings, and he was urged to yield to the decision of the assembly, whatever it might be; but he nobly declared,

"I am ready to be instructed by the council; but I beseech and conjure you by Him who is the God of us all, that you do not force me to what I cannot do without contradicting my conscience, and without danger of eternal damnation. . . . . As, now, many articles have been imputed to me, which to hold or to teach never entered my thoughts, how can I renounce them by an oath? But as regards those articles which really belong to me, I will cheerfully do what you require, if any one can persuade me to another opinion."

"Recant, or die," was, however, the ultimatum of the council, fully concurred in by the emperor. The former Huss could not do, unless convinced by the Word of God of his error. The latter he could and did do nobly.

When the flames had done their work, the ashes of this faithful witness were thrown into the Rhine, that they might not "pollute the earth."

The spot where the execution is supposed to have taken place is now marked by a simple monument, bearing the inscription, "Joannes Hus, *exustus non convictus*"—"John Huss, burned, but not convicted." His real crime was putting the authority of the Holy Scriptures above that of the church—of Christ above that of the pope. The Church of Rome cannot tolerate such doctrine. To admit it would seal her own dissolution.

It is worthy of note that after the removal of Huss to the Franciscan convent in Constance, where his trial took place, his enemy Balthasar Cossa, the ex-Pope John XXIII., having been deposed by the council and accused of abominable crimes, was himself closely confined in the same castle of Gottleben in which Huss had suffered so much.

JEROME OF PRAGUE.

The Council of Constance was opened Nov. 5, 1414, and closed April 22, 1418. There were present at it some thirty cardinals, twenty archbishops, one hundred and fifty bishops, three patriarchs, and numerous abbots, monks, and priests; and, in addition to these clerical members, it was attended by the Emperor Sigismund and the ambassadors of several kings, and by princes, dukes, barons, knights, and delegates from universities. It was an imposing assembly : it had numbers, wealth, power, and a large amount of learning ; but, judging from its actions, it had little of the grace of God, and no adequate knowledge of the doctrines of God's holy Word. It condemned the works of Wickliffe, and sentenced John Huss to be burned; and in less than one year after the execution of Huss, Jerome, by order of this same council, was led out and consumed by the flames for attesting the truths of the gospel.

The subject of our sketch was born at Prague, of a knightly family, about 1375, some six years later than his friend and teacher John Huss. He is called Jerome of Prague to distinguish him from one of the Latin Fathers of the same name, the author of the Latin translation of the Old Testament called the Vulgate. Of Jerome's early youth we know but little; but evidently he had a great desire for learning, so that he pursued his studies first at the university of his native city, then at Heidelberg, at Cologne, at Paris, and at Oxford, and finally obtained such a reputation for scholarship as led the king of Poland, in 1410, to invite him to organize the newly projected university of Cracow. While at Oxford he embraced the doctrines of Wickliffe, and it is said that he transcribed several of his writings and took them back with him to Prague. It is also said that, by his advocacy of the English reformer's principles at Paris, he aroused the dangerous opposition of Gerson, the chancellor of the French university, who was afterwards a leading member of the council which condemned him.

After his return to Prague, about 1407, he became associated with Huss in the university, and aided him largely in bringing about the change in the distribution of votes which secured the control of the institution to Bohemia. But this measure gave great offence to the German members of the university, who had bound themselves by a solemn oath to withdraw if their privileges were curtailed; and the charge of having sent away the Germans was afterwards brought against both Jerome and Huss on their trial at Constance.

Jerome was not content with advocating his new views in his native place; he took long journeys to propagate that faith which was now so precious to him, and on more than one of these journeys he was seized and imprisoned for a time.

Finally, his opposition assumed marvellous boldness, when the strength of the Romish party is taken into account. In a public discussion held in 1412 he took part on the side of Huss against the papal bull lately issued, closing his argument with the words, "Whoever holds with us, let him follow us. Huss and myself will go to the council-house, and tell the council boldly to their face that the papal bull and indulgences are iniquitous."

Some two years after this, when Huss was called to leave Prague and to present himself before the council at Constance, he was addressed by Jerome as follows: "Dear master, stand firm; maintain bravely what you have written and preached against the pride, avarice and other vices of the churchmen, with argument drawn from the Holy Scriptures. Should this task become too severe for thee—should I learn that thou hast fallen into any peril, I will fly at once to thy assistance."

Sooner than he expected, probably, Jerome was called to make good his promise. In 1415, while Huss was imprisoned in Constance, Jerome hastened to see him, and, if possible, to aid him in his sore trouble. He soon found, however, that he could do nothing to help his friend, and that his own liberty and life were in danger. Therefore, by the advice of friends, he left the city and went to Ueberlingen, on the northern shore of the Lake of Constance, whence he wrote soliciting a safe-conduct; but instead of being furnished with one, he was cited to appear before the council and answer certain charges. Yielding again to the entreaty of friends, Jerome then turned his face towards his native Bohemia, where he would have been safe; but on the 24th of April, 1415, after having publicly expressed his indignation at the injustice of the council, he was arrested and imprisoned, at the instigation of the priest in the village of Hirschau, in Swabia. From there, loaded with chains, he was taken, May 23d, to Constance, and dragged through the city in triumph.

The council was much excited at the news of his arrest and arrival. Many of its members had in former days been overpowered by his eloquence and shamed by his exposure of their character and principles, and now anticipated their revenge. Even Chancellor Gerson could not restrain himself, but said to him, "Jerome, when you came to Paris you fancied yourself, with your eloquence, to be an angel of light."

Jerome was now imprisoned, and Huss, finding it out, sent an old servant to him with the message, "Strengthen thy soul; be mindful of that truth which thou hadst so often in thy mouth when thou wast at liberty and thy limbs were free from shackles. Do not fear to face death for it."

Six weeks after this Huss was burned, and poor Jerome, eloquent in speech, but filled with fear at such a terrible death, and worn by his own cruel confinement, was soon after taken before the council, where, step by step, he yielded and explained, until, on the 23d of September, he finally read a recantation prepared for him by Cardinal Cambray, and ended with the words, "I moreover swear, by the Holy Trinity and by these most holy Gospels, that I will abide in the truth of the Catholic Church; and I do pronounce all those that shall contravene this faith with their dogmas worthy of eternal anathema," etc.

If Jerome thought to escape the clutches of Rome by such concession, he was sadly mistaken. If his offence had been theft or murder, he might have obtained his release; but to teach that it was a question "whether the pope possessed more power than any other priest," could not then, and indeed would not now, be tolerated in the Romish Church.

Though even the commissioners who had conducted Jerome's trial acknowledged that by his recantation he had earned a right to be set at liberty, his Bohemian opposers urged that if allowed to return home he would again occasion disturbances by advocating the doctrines which he had lately abjured; and Jerome, though no longer closely fettered, was still kept in a noisome and dark prison, where he could not see to read or write.

Finally, new charges were formulated against him, and a new commission was appointed to examine him. But after some progress had been made in this second trial, he demanded a public examination, and on the 23d and 26th of May, 1416, from 7 A. M. to 1 P. M., he was permitted to defend himself before the assembled council. During the dreary months that had followed his recantation, the truths which he had formerly maintained had, doubtless, regained their power over his conscience and affections. After having, with admirable skill and eloquence, answered all the charges brought against him, he surprised the council by boldly passing in review the victims of unjust accusation and hierarchical hate both in pagan and Christian times, classing his beloved Huss among the number, and confessing, "Of all the sins that I have committed since my youth, none weigh so heavily upon my mind, to cause me such poignant remorse, as that which I committed in this fatal place, when I approved of the iniquitous sentence rendered against Wickliffe, and against the holy martyr John Huss, my master and friend."

Then, facing his judges, he exclaimed, "I trust in God ... that one day ... you shall see Jerome ... summoning you all to judgment, and then you must render your account to God and to me, if you have proceeded against me wrongfully."

This defiance made the fatal issue of the trial a certainty, and though the accused had, by the evidences of his sufferings and by his eloquence and wisdom, won the sympathy of many in the council, so that a respite for reflection was granted him, repeated efforts to persuade him to a second recantation having proved unavailing, the 30th of May was appointed for the delivery and execution of his sentence.

On this day, in reply to the bishop's discourse setting forth the charges, Jerome again defended himself, and rebuked the vices of the clergy.

His sentence was then read, a paper cap, covered with pictures of devils in flames, was placed upon his head, and he was turned over to the civil authorities to be burned.

Surrounded by a company of soldiers, he was led out to meet his sad fate. When he arrived at the place of execution, where Huss had suffered before him, he knelt and prayed. While he was being fastened to the stake he sang a hymn. Then, having bidden the executioner light the fire before his eyes instead of behind him, declaring that had he been afraid of the flames he would not have been there, he addressed the multitude of spectators, and in a few words reaffirmed his belief in the gospel truths which he had sung, and in the injustice of the execution of Huss. His last audible words were, "Lord God, have pity on me; forgive me my sins, for thou knowest that I have sincerely loved thy truth."

Thus humbly and penitently, yet bravely and rejoicingly, died Jerome, enabled by his divine Master to overcome that natural fear of a horrible death which at first had proved a snare to him. Even Poggio, the orator of the council, wrote that "with cheerful looks he went readily and willingly to his death. No stoic ever suffered death with so firm a soul as Jerome."

His ashes were carted away and thrown into

the Rhine; but they will be gathered again when Christ his Lord shall come. The advocate is now silenced, but the cause lives, and will finally triumph over all opposers. Meantime, it is true, as Dr. Mears so well states in his "Heroes of Bohemia" (the volume to which we are chiefly indebted for the facts of our sketch), "The most illustrious names in the great Council of Constance are scarcely known beyond the circles of antiquarian research, or the northwest lines of Romish exclusivism; but Jerome and Huss shine in the light of that great Reformation which they anticipated by a century."

PATRICK HAMILTON.

ON the 1st of March, 1528, some eight years before Tyndale was betrayed by a Romish spy, Archbishop Beaton condemned Patrick Hamilton to be burned because he advocated the doctrines of the Reformation, and exposed the errors of popery. How he came to embrace these doctrines, then so much opposed by the papal church, will appear as we proceed with our sketch.

Patrick Hamilton was born at Stonehouse, near Glasgow, Scotland, in the year 1504. His father was a knight of some fame, and his mother was a granddaughter of James II. of Scotland. In accordance with the custom of those days, Patrick was appointed titular abbot of Ferne, in Ross-shire when but a boy of thirteen. Apparently at about the same time, 1517, he went to study in Paris, where he graduated in 1520. Afterwards visiting Louvain, in the Netherlands, he probably came under the influence of Erasmus. In 1523, having returned to Scotland, he connected himself with the university of St. Andrews, and became a member of its faculty of arts in the following year.

He was now an ardent supporter of the Reformed doctrines, and labored to spread them among his countrymen. Before long his evangelical preaching attracted the attention of Archbishop Beaton, who in the beginning of 1527 ordered that he should be charged with heresy. Hamilton avoided a trial at this time by escaping to Germany.

Reaching Wittenberg, he listened to the teachings of Luther and Melancthon, and afterward went to Marburg, where he entered his name as a student in the new university just opened by Philip, landgrave of Hesse. The teacher to whom he particularly attached himself here was Francis Lambert, a Frenchman by birth, and formerly a Carthusian monk, enthusiastic in devotion to his order, but who had been converted by the writings of Luther to the simple faith of the gospel. Lambert, becoming interested in his pupil, put him forward, notwithstanding his youth, as a teacher in the university, and Hamilton there maintained with more than ordinary power the doctrines of the reformers. There, also, he wrote a treatise on the law and the gospel, which was afterwards known by the title of "Patrick's Places." And there, too, he held intercourse with Frith and Tyndale.

But it was with him as with Patrick: he con-

PATRICK HAMILTON. 57

tinually heard a voice calling to him from his native land, "Come back; we are perishing for lack of knowledge." Doubtless, the Spirit of God was leading him to his field of labor and suffering.

Accordingly, in the autumn of 1527 he left his many friends and the privileges of the Marburg university, and returned to his native land. Arriving in Scotland he repaired to his brother's residence at Kincavel, near Linlithgow, and commenced with renewed zeal the work of preaching the gospel and of exposing the errors of Rome. At this time, following the example of several of the great German reformers, he practically repudiated the Romish doctrine of the celibacy of the clergy, by marrying a young lady, whose name, though she belonged to a noble family, has been lost to the historian.

But his active work was not long to be continued. Popery had too strong a hold, especially among the ruling powers of the nation, to allow itself to be uprooted without a determined defence. Accordingly, Hamilton was summoned to St. Andrew's by Archbishop Beaton; and although he felt that bonds and imprisonment awaited him, he determined to go, that even in the midst of his enemies he might witness for Christ. There opportunity was given him to dispute with friars, and to advocate his opinions concerning the reforms which in his judgment were necessary to be carried out in the church. But this liberty was allowed him for the purpose of securing charges against him; and as soon as these were formulated he was put upon his trial, the charges being preferred by a Dominican friar named Campbell.

The principal accusations were that he taught that it was proper for the people to read God's Word, and that it was useless to offer masses for the souls of the dead. Hamilton admitted the truth of these charges, and boldly defended his doctrine. But his judges, Archbishop Beaton and the bishops and clergy associated with him in council, could not endure the truths presented by their prisoner, which indeed were greatly to their disadvantage; for a people before whom an open Bible is spread will soon test by it the lives and teachings of their pastors, and to abolish masses for the dead is to cut off a chief source of the revenues of Rome's priesthood. Hamilton therefore was quickly condemned, and in a few hours afterwards, to avoid any possibility of his rescue by influential friends, the stake was prepared before the gate of St. Salvador College.

When the martyr was brought to the stake, he removed his outer garments and gave them to his servant, with the words, "These will not profit me in the fire, but they will profit thee. Hereafter thou canst have no profit from me except the example of my death, which I pray thee keep in memory, for, though bitter to the flesh and fearful before man, it is the door of eternal life, which none will attain who denies Christ Jesus before this ungodly generation."

His agony was prolonged by a slow fire, so that his execution lasted some six hours; but, through it all, he manifested true heroism and unshaken faith in the truth of the doctrines which he preached. His last words were, "How long, O Lord, shall darkness brood over this realm? How long wilt thou suffer this tyranny of man? Lord Jesus, receive my spirit."

Thus, in the bloom of early manhood, died Scotland's first Reformation martyr, and his death was not in vain. A Romanist afterwards said, "The smoke of Patrick Hamilton infected all that it blew upon." His mouth was closed, but the story of his death was repeated by a thousand tongues. It emboldened others to seek a martyr's crown, and stirred up many more to defend the truths for which he died, and to repudiate the hierarchy which found it necessary to defend itself by such means. "Humanly speaking," says the author of "The Champions of the Reformation," to whom we are chiefly indebted for the facts of our sketch, "could there have been found a fitter apostle for ignorant, benighted Scotland, than this eloquent, fervent, pious man? Endowed with all those gifts that sway the heads of the masses, a zealous, pious laborer in season and out of season, what herculean labors might he not have accomplished! What signal triumphs might he not have achieved! So men may reason, but God judged otherwise. A short trial, a brief essay in the work he loved and longed for, was permitted to him, and then the goodly vessel, still in sight of land, was broken in pieces."

HUGH LATIMER.

ON the 16th of October, 1555, some three years before the death of England's "bloody Mary," there were to be seen, outside of the gate of Bocardo jail at Oxford, and opposite Balliol College, two piles of fagots, which were soon to be kindled. In the midst of each a man stood bound. One, feeble in health and bearing the weight of sixty-five years, but yet undaunted in spirit, was heard to encourage his fellow-sufferer with the words, "Be of good comfort, Master Ridley, and play the man; we shall this day light such a candle, by God's grace, in England, as I trust shall never be put out." This noble man was Hugh Latimer, "the John Knox of England."

Latimer was the son of a farmer in Leicestershire. He was born about 1490, and educated in the university of Cambridge, which he entered the same year (1505) in which Luther entered the convent of Erfurt. In his youth he was, to use his own words, an "obstinate papist," and by his zeal earned the position of cross-bearer in the church processions. At his graduation in the divinity school his oration was directed against Melancthon. The ability he displayed in defence of the Romish doctrine attracted the attention of Bilney, who had by this time obtained the light and life which are revealed in Christ, and which he found, not by masses, penances, or fastings, but by the revelation of God in his Word. "This is a faithful saying, and worthy of all acceptation, that Christ Jesus came into the world to save sinners," was the message which the Holy Spirit used to bring to his soul a sense of pardon and peace; and he longed to tell his experience to this zealous, talented student, who had displayed such ignorance of this precious truth in his oration against Melancthon. Accordingly, he went to Latimer and begged him to hear his confession, which the young priest agreed to do; and in one of his sermons he afterwards declared that by that confession he learned more than he had done for many years; from that time forward "he began to search the Word of God, and forsook the school doctors and fooleries." Soon afterwards he defended the truth from the pulpit as zealously as he had formerly opposed it.

One of his hearers, Thomas Bacon, afterwards wrote concerning the commotion thus produced in Oxford, "None but the stiff-necked and uncircumcised in heart went away from his sermons without being affected with high detestation of sin, and moved to all godliness and virtue. I did know certain men which, through the persuasion of their friends, went unto his sermons swelling, blown full, and puffed up like unto Æsop's frog, with envy and malice against him; but when they returned, the sermon being done, and were demanded how they liked him and his doctrine, they answered, with the bishops and Pharisees' servants, 'There was never man that spake like unto this man.'"

Such preaching could not escape the notice of Latimer's superiors, and he was forbidden by the bishop of Ely, whom he had displeased by a sermon contrasting English prelates with Christ, to preach any more in the university churches. He was finally brought before Wolsey, who, however, gave him a license to preach anywhere.

Two sermons, preached in 1529, in which Latimer urged that the people should have the Scriptures in English, again involved him in difficulty; but an investigation resulted merely in binding both him and his opponents not to use "offensive expressions against each other in the pulpit."

In 1530, Thomas Cromwell, Wolsey's agent, and his successor in the favor of Henry VIII., recommended Latimer to the king, and he was made royal chaplain, and soon after appointed to the living of West Kington in Wiltshire. But his zeal in his Master's work did not permit him to restrict himself to his own parish; he travelled far and near, preaching the truth; and, as a consequence, he was summoned in 1532 to appear before the bishop of London and other clergy to render an account of his doings. He was condemned and afterwards excommunicated, but, by favor of the king, was restored, after making some slight concessions and confessions, and allowed to return to his parish again.

Soon afterwards the archbishop of Canterbury died, and Cranmer was appointed in his place. He remembered his former fellow-student at Cambridge, recalled Latimer to his court chaplaincy, so that Henry VIII. heard him preach every Wednesday during Lent in 1534, and in the fall of 1535 Latimer was consecrated bishop of Worcester.

The following year, at a convocation of the clergy, Latimer, by request of Cranmer, opened the convocation with two sermons, which are still in existence, and are supposed to equal in boldness anything that John Knox ever proclaimed from the pulpit, though the preacher no doubt knew that many of his audience would have rejoiced to see him bound to the stake.

In 1539, after several years of faithful episcopal work, Latimer was arrested and forced to resign his see, because he did not approve of the six anti-reformation articles drawn up by Henry VIII. He was soon released, but towards the close of Henry's reign was again condemned for heresy and sent to the Tower of London, where he remained until the accession of Edward VI. When released, his diocese was offered him again, but he declined it, probably on account of failing health, which, however, did not prevent him from preaching the gospel often before the court, and as opportunity offered throughout the kingdom.

Edward died, however, and was succeeded by Mary, a bigoted Catholic; and Latimer, having refused to escape, though warning was given him of his danger, was soon arrested and sent again to the Tower, where he was kept "without fire in the frosty winter," so that he "well nigh starved with cold." Yet even these hardships did not destroy the natural buoyancy of his spirits, and he used to jest with his keeper about the chance of cheating his persecutors "if they did not look better to him."

In April, 1554, he was transferred to Oxford, together with Cranmer and Ridley, where he remained in prison for more than a year, being occasionally brought before certain commissioners for examination, with a view to securing a recantation of his principles; but in spite of all threats and persuasions he nobly maintained the truth. His appearance at an examination held in September, 1555, is described by Fox as follows:

"Suffering and poverty were depicted in his appearance as he bowed before the commissioners, holding his hat in his hand, with a kerchief bound round his head, and upon it a nightcap or two, such as horsemen used in those days, with two broad flaps to button under the chin. He wore an old threadbare Bristol frieze gown, girdled to his body with a penny leathern girdle; his Testament was suspended from this girdle by a leather sling, and his spectacles, without a case, hung from his neck upon his breast."

Notwithstanding his feebleness, when he was urged to admit the doctrine of the papacy, his old fire was aroused and he replied with energy, appealing to the Scriptures as the coin "which should not be clipped," and which needed "no gelding."

The result was that he was condemned to die—for Rome had no mercy for the man who appealed to the Scriptures against her authority—and the scene already described took place. The site is now marked by a noble monument.

Tullock (to whose essay we are chiefly indebted for the facts in this sketch), says of him, "Nothing is more remarkable in him than his cheerfulness. Ill in body, tried and persecuted and cast down by many troubles, he is always cheerful; cheerful at Cambridge, amid the scowls of friars; cheerful in his parish under episcopal frowns, and in his diocese amid an obtuse and opposing clergy; cheerful in the Tower, when nearly starved to death with cold; cheerful at the stake in the thought of the illuminating blaze that he and Ridley would make for the glory of the gospel and the happiness of England. An earnest, hopeful, and happy man, honest, fearless, open-hearted, hating nothing but baseness, and fearing none but God; not throwing away his life, yet not counting it dear; when the great crisis came, calmly yielding it up as the crown of his long sacrifice and struggle. There may be other reformers that more engage our admiration; there is no one that more excites our love."

MARTIN LUTHER.

In the Augustinian convent of Erfurt, between the years 1505 and 1508, might be seen, three times a day, a young monk, praying with intense sincerity to some one of twenty saints whom he had chosen as the objects of his devotion, having divided them into classes, so that he might pray to each once a week. He was enthusiastic in his devotion to the papal church, and fully believed that salvation could be secured only through strict obedience to its commands—by the performance of "good works," such as prayers, watchings, and fastings. But his conscience, even then enlightened by earnest study of the Scriptures, too clearly discerned his own sinfulness and the perfect holiness required by God, to be quieted by all his efforts. The peace he so much desired came not to him.

After a while, however, a fellow-monk whispered in his ear, "Christ is a real Saviour for real sinners;" and that brought peace to his soul. The truth was the seed-wheat of the Reformation dropped into Luther's heart, and by-and-by it brought forth abundant fruit. It was another form of stating the doctrine of justification by faith in Christ Jesus, which Luther afterwards declared to be "the article of a standing or a falling church."

But how came Luther to be in this convent? And how did he afterwards use the important knowledge gained there? These are the questions which we purpose answering in our present sketch.

Martin Luther was born at Eisleben, a village of Lower Saxony, November 10, 1483, nearly four hundred years ago. His father, Hans Luther, was a poor miner in the village of Moehra, but subsequently removed to the town of Mansfeld, where his circumstances improved, and he determined to educate his oldest son Martin to be a lawyer. That determination did not mean, as with us, that he would provide the means necessary, but only that he would not demand his time at some money-making work.

Accordingly, when nearly fourteen years of age, Luther was removed from Mansfeld, where his teacher had helped to train the future hero to the endurance of hardness, by once giving him fifteen floggings in a forenoon, and was sent to Magdeburg, to a somewhat celebrated school, where the boys paid their own way by collecting alms from the citizens, under whose windows they were accustomed to sing twice a week. From this school he was transferred to one at Eisenach, where he supported himself in the same manner. It was here that his sad face and sweet voice attracted the attention of that noble woman, Ursula Cotta, in whose house he found a happy home. Here he continued until the completion of his eighteenth year, when he entered the university at Erfurt, and distinguished himself there by his application and attainments. It is said that he began every day with prayer to God, and that he declared that "To pray well is the better half of study."

Some two years after he entered the university, he discovered in its library a Latin Bible, the first he had ever seen, which he read with intense delight. Soon after his graduation as Master of Arts, in 1505, his strong desire to possess a personal assurance of the favor of God was intensified by the sudden death of a dear college friend, and by his own apparently narrow escape from lightning. Believing that the holiness and peace for which he longed could be attained in a monastic life, he entered the Augustinian convent, where, as we have said, he was diligent in prayer to the saints, but where he soon found "the real Saviour for real sinners."

Being recommended by his friend Staupitz,

the vicar-general of the Augustinians in Germany, to Frederick, elector of Saxony, he was appointed by that prince to the chair of metaphysics in the new university of Wittenberg. He accepted the appointment, and began his great work. Here he lectured, preached, and wrote many of his books; and though he died while absent on a mission at Eisleben, here he was buried; and in the market-place of the town a bronze statue reminds the citizens of the esteem in which he was held by Germany.

At the request of the Council of Wittenberg, Luther soon added the labors of a preacher and pastor in one of the churches to the duties of a professor in the university, and many flocked to hear his sermons. In 1510 he was sent to Rome on business connected with the Augustinian order. He approached the city with feelings of the utmost reverence for it as the residence of the visible head of the church; he left it with eyes opened to the abuses with which the clergy had filled it, and yet without withdrawing his allegiance from the pope.

In 1512 he began, as Doctor of Biblical Theology, to lecture on the Bible before the students in the university, his aim, in lecture or sermon, being always to lead his hearers to that faith in Christ by which he now lived.

At length came the memorable year in which he was brought face to face with the evils of the indulgence system, and roused to oppose it. Persons who were accustomed to confess their sins to him and to receive spiritual direction from him, approached his confessional avowing themselves guilty of terrible sins, but exhibiting letters of indulgence which they had brought from the Dominican monk Tetzel, and announcing their determination to continue in their transgressions. Luther, horror-struck at such impiety, warned them that no human promise of salvation could shield them from divine justice without their repentance. Nor was he satisfied with these private admonitions. He preached a sermon in which he exposed the wickedness of Tetzel's traffic, and the worthlessness of his indulgences, and advised all to abstain from buying them.

Another and still bolder step he took.

It was on October 31st, 1517, that Luther nailed his ninety-five theses to the door of the elector's new church at Wittenberg, and thereby entered his public protest against the sale of indulgences, and also against some of the doctrines of the Romish Church, which gave them support. We quote the 1st, 6th, and 36th of these celebrated theses:

"1. When our Lord and Master Jesus Christ says, 'Repent,' he means that the whole life of his faithful servants upon earth shall be a constant and perpetual repentance.

"6. The pope cannot remit any condemnation, but can only declare and confirm the remission of God, except in the cases that appertain to himself; if he does otherwise, the condemnation remains the same.

"36. Every Christian who truly repents of his sins, enjoys an entire remission, both of the penalties and of the guilt, without any need of indulgences."

These theses were printed and circulated all over Germany in fourteen days. Everywhere they excited attention. Some souls, enlightened by the Holy Spirit, rejoiced that one man was found with boldness sufficient to oppose the iniquitous traffic. Others, among them high dignitaries of the church, whose support Luther had hoped for, believing that Tetzel had overleaped his instructions, discouraged discussion of the topics of the theses as useless and imprudent, or condemned it as rebellion against the church's authority.

Many were the attacks made, in writing, upon Luther. Tetzel answered his theses with a set of theses of his own, which the students of

Wittenberg burned. The inquisitor James von Hoogstraten begged of the pope that Luther might be burned, but Leo X. himself was at first inclined to treat the affair as a monkish quarrel. Luther, with his veneration for the pope still unshaken, wrote a humble letter of appeal to him; but before this reached the pontiff, Leo, convinced that the papacy had in the Augustinian monk a more dangerous foe than he had at first imagined, ordered him, by a summons which reached him August 7th, 1518, to appear before the papal court at Rome and answer for his conduct.

By the influence of the elector Frederick, Luther was saved from thus walking into the jaws of death, and Cardinal Cajetan was, as the pope's nuncio, appointed to receive his submission at Augsburg. But the wily cardinal found that neither persuasions nor threats would move "little brother Martin" to submit, unless his errors could be pointed out from the Scriptures. He accordingly dismissed him, and told his friends, "I do n't want to talk more with this beast. He has a deep eye, and marvellous speculations in his head."

From fury and violence Luther made his escape back to Wittenberg, after having written an appeal from "Leo X. ill informed, to Leo X.

better informed," which appeal was fastened to the door of the cathedral after his departure.

The death of the emperor of Germany, by which Luther's friend Frederick became for the time the acting emperor, and other complications, secured the safety of Luther until the Diet of Worms. Here the new emperor, Charles V., cited him to appear and undergo examination as to his teachings; and although many of his friends feared the result of his appearance, they could not persuade him to absent himself. His answer to the remonstrances of one of them was, "Though there were as many devils in Worms as there are tiles on the houses, still I would go."

By degrees new light had entered his mind, so that he no longer regarded the pope as the vicar of Christ, but rather as Antichrist. Accordingly, some time before this, he wrote, "I despise the fury of Rome and contemn her favor. No more reconciliation; no more communication with her for ever. Let her condemn me; let her burn my writings. In my turn I will condemn and publicly burn the pontifical law, that nest of every heresy. The moderation I have hitherto shown has been unavailing. I now renounce it."

These brave words brought him letters of

commendation from many men of influence, and emboldened him to publish, in June, 1520, an "Appeal to his Imperial Majesty, and the Christian Nobility of the German Nation, on the Reformation of Christianity." This is said to be "one of the most eloquent and magnificent of his writings," and to have aroused to white heat the people of Germany against the pope; so that his bulls no longer filled them with terror, but rather with contempt. The pamphlet, among other things, assailed the sacerdotal caste, as follows: "It has been said that the pope, the bishops, and the priests, and all those who people the convents, form the ecclesiastical or spiritual state, and that the princes, the nobility, the citizens, the peasants, form the secular or lay estates. This is a fine story. Let no one, however, be grieved. All Christians belong to the spiritual state, and there is no other difference between them than that which arises from the functions which they discharge. We have all one baptism, one faith, and it is this which constitutes the spiritual man. The unction, the tonsure, the cowl, ordination, consecration by a bishop or the pope, may make a hypocrite; they cannot of themselves make a Christian. . . . If we possess not the divine consecration, the pope's anointing can never make a priest."

In the fall of 1520, soon after the publication of this appeal, the bull of Leo X., condemning the writings of Luther to the flames, and ordering that, unless he should recant within sixty days, his person should be seized and sent to Rome, was published in Germany. But instead of evoking respect and obedience, the bull excited general indignation and ridicule. Luther, undismayed by it, wrote "Against the bull of Antichrist," appealed from the pope to a general council, and signified his final rupture with the papal see by publicly burning the recent bull and the pontifical laws, December 10th, 1520.

But the time of the meeting of the Diet of Worms arrived, and there Luther appeared, single-handed, to contend with more than an empire. The diet was opened by the new emperor, Charles, in January, 1521. The 16th of the following April, Luther arrived in the city, and next day he was cited "to appear before his imperial majesty and the states of the empire." He appeared, and was asked two questions: 1. "Do you acknowledge yourself the author of these writings?" 2. "Will you retract the doctrines therein taught?" To the first he replied, after the titles were read, "Yes, they are mine." To the second he answered that unless these doctrines were shown to be contrary to the Word of God, he could not retract them. He said, "I put no faith in the mere authority of the pontiff or of councils, which have often been mistaken, and which have frequently contradicted one another. I recognize no other guide than the Bible—the Word of God. Unless convicted of error by that, I cannot and will not retract, for we must never act contrary to our conscience."

This august assembly could neither cajole nor frighten the humble monk from adherence to the Word of God as the supreme rule for man's faith and life. He was permitted to leave the city on account of having before his appearance obtained from the emperor a safe-conduct. But on May 26 he was placed under the ban of the empire. The sentence of the diet ran as follows: "The Augustinian monk, Martin Luther, notwithstanding our exhortation, has rushed like a madman on our holy church, and has attempted to destroy it by books overflowing with blasphemy. . . . For this reason, under pain of incurring the penalties of high treason, we forbid you to harbor the said Luther after the appointed time shall have expired, to conceal him, to give him food or drink, or to furnish him by word or act, publicly or secretly, with any kind of succor whatsoever. We enjoin you, moreover, to seize him, or cause him to be seized, wherever you may find him, and bring him before us without delay," etc.

On the publication of this edict, Rome shouted for joy. The dignitaries of the church thought the end of the controversy had come, and that no one would dare befriend the poor monk, in opposition not only to the pope's bull but to the emperor's edict. They did not consider that God has the hearts of all men in his hand, and can easily raise up defenders for his faithful servants.

This was the experience of Luther; for as he reached the Thuringian forest, on his return from Worms, he was seized by masked horsemen and carried a prisoner to the Wartburg, a strong fortress situated on a mountain and surrounded by forests. The seeming violence of his abduction was in reality the loving force of friends, who in this way would protect the champion of the gospel against papal bull and imperial ban. Here Luther, disguised as a knight, and known to the attendants of the castle as "Knight George," passed many months; and from here, though suffering from physical ailments and mental conflicts and depression, he soon "inundated Germany with his writings"—among them treatises against indulgences, the confessional, and monastic vows.

Here he also made the first draft of his translation of the New Testament, which he afterwards published in 1522, and in little over a year several editions of it were called for, such was the desire of the people to possess a copy of the Word of God in their own tongue. His translation of the Old Testament was completed and published after some thirteen years' labor, the entire Bible being issued in 1534.

At the end of ten months, such was the condition of things at Wittenberg in Luther's absence, that at the risk of his life he left his safe retreat and returned to his old field of labor. At this, and the subsequent period of his life, he endured many trials, some of them from the conduct of loved friends, such as Carlstadt and Erasmus; but he boldly maintained the truth, as he understood it; and during this period he made much progress in the divine life and in the knowledge of God's requirements of men.

On June 13, 1525, he married Catharine von Bora, an escaped nun, an event over which his enemies rejoiced as a manifest token of his apostasy from true religion, but which proved, in its results, a wise step, and was the source of great comfort to Luther during the later period of his life.

The emperor's hands being full, with the conduct of his disagreements with Francis I. and the pope, and the empire being further disquieted by the Turks' invasion of Hungary, the Reformation was allowed to sweep on in full tide. But hostilities having been in some degree suspended, it was decreed at the second Diet of Spires, which convened March 15, 1529, that the German states should obey the edict promulgated at Worms against Luther and his doctrines. Against this proceeding the friends of the Reformation united in a protest, from which fact they and those who held their opinions were ever after called Protestants.

In June, 1530, a diet was opened at Augsburg to concert measures against the Turks, and to settle the religious dissensions of the empire. Luther, on account of the sentence of outlawry still hanging over him, was not permitted by his friends to be present; but by his letters to Melanchthon and others he doubtless exerted a large influence. The Augsburg Confession, prepared by Melanchthon and setting forth the religious belief of the Lutherans, was presented to the diet, but, as a matter of course, not approved by that assembly, and the result was the League of Schmalkald, formed in March, 1531, by which the protesting princes and cities bound themselves together to defend Protestantism by force of arms, if needful.

For some fifteen years from this period Luther continued with little molestation in his arduous labors, caring for all the churches, and exhorting and warning them by his pamphlets and books. Being called by Count Albert of Mansfeld in January, 1546, to Eisleben, to act as arbitrator in matters of difference between him and Count Gebhard, he undertook the journey and succeeded in his mission, but was taken sick, and died, February 8, 1546, in the same town where, nearly sixty-three years before, he had first seen the light of a world in which he did so grand a work.

In a letter to a friend, written a few weeks before his death, he expressed some natural weariness under the burdens of age and the incessant labors of his busy life, but concluded joyfully, "However, Christ is all in all to me; he can and does do all things for me. Praise be to him eternally." In the same spirit, when dying, he committed his soul to his Heavenly Father, with a hearty and happy trust in Christ his Redeemer, whose eternal praise he doubtless still shows forth.

His body was conveyed to Wittenberg, and now sleeps "at the foot of the pulpit from which the thunders of his eloquence had so often shaken Christendom."

PHILIP MELANCHTHON.

On the 21st of April, 1560, a funeral procession passed along the streets of Wittenberg, composed of professors, councillors, noblemen, students, and citizens, all deeply moved, and many in tears. They were bearing to a tomb, by the side of the lamented Luther, his friend Melanchthon, the "teacher of Germany," "the flower," as a loving pupil said, "out of which many bees have sipped and made honey for the comfort and instruction of Christendom.

This remarkable man was born on the 16th of February, 1497, in the town of Bretten, in the Palatinate, now included in the Grand Duchy of Baden. His father was a celebrated armorer, patronized by the German emperor Maximilian. His mother was noted for her piety; and the familiar adage, "Alms do not impoverish," was with her an original and favorite motto. Philip was the oldest son. He soon manifested a special taste for acquiring languages, and showed more than ordinary logical ability.

At ten years of age he was deprived by death of his beloved father, who said to Philip, as the boy stood by his bed, two days before he died, "I have experienced many changes in this world, but greater ones are coming. I counsel thee, my son, to fear God and live honestly." These words were treasured in Philip's memory as long as he lived.

At about this time he was sent to a Latin school at Pforzheim, where his uncle, John Reuchlin, the celebrated scholar, took a great interest in him on account of his talents, and translated his German name Schwartzerd, which means *black earth*, into the Greek Melanchthon, by which he was afterwards known.

In October, 1509, he entered the university of Heidelberg. Here he greatly distinguished himself by his proficiency in the ancient languages, so that when a professor was considering a very difficult question in the class-room one day, and exclaimed, "Where shall I find a Grecian?" the students with one voice replied, "Melanchthon." After graduating as bachelor of arts at Heidelberg when only fourteen, he attended the university of Tübingen, where, in 1514, he took the degree of master of arts, which gave him the privilege of delivering lectures. He won great applause as a lecturer, and was recommended to Elector Frederick by Reuchlin for a professorship in the university at Wittenberg. Melanchthon reached his new field of labor in August, 1518. Here he was to meet Luther and be associated with him in the great work of his life. The two were complements of each other, and both were needed for the work now, in the providence of God, to be accomplished in Germany.

A few days after the arrival of the new professor of Greek at Wittenberg, he delivered a lecture introductory to his course. Luther was among his auditory, and wrote to Spalatin, the elector's chaplain, "Philip delivered a very learned and chaste address on the fourth day after his arrival, and that, too, with such applause and admiration on every side that you need not trouble yourself farther in commending him to us. We must look away from his exterior appearance; we rejoice in his gifts at the same time that we are amazed at them." Melanchthon was very small and boyish-looking in person, though a "giant in intellect and learning," as one of his contemporaries said.

An important part in the history of the Reformation had now been reached. Even at Rome the controversy was no longer regarded as a mere dispute among the monks, but as one involving the very existence of the church. Luther and Melanchthon labored side by side, with an honest purpose to know and hold to the truth. The university was crowded with students from all parts of Germany, and thus the instrumentality for diffusing Reformation principles was easily found.

In 1519 Melanchthon took the degree of bachelor of divinity, and from that time devoted himself mainly to studying and teaching theology; though he never was ordained, and would not accept the title of doctor of theology. In 1521 he published his "Loci Communes," a volume on the doctrines of the Bible, which met with an almost unprecedented circulation, and did much to promote a knowledge of Bible doctrine. It is said to have passed through more than fifty editions during the author's life. In addition to other literary works, Melanchthon gave Luther important help in the translation of the Bible.

In 1520 Melanchthon married the daughter of burgomaster Crapp of Wittenberg. As he was not a priest, this did not produce the opposition which Luther's marriage, some years later, did.

At the Diet of Spires, Melanchthon took the lead in the discussions, Luther being absent. Here, on the 20th of April, 1529, the celebrated protest and appeal was entered which gave the name of Protestants to the opposers of Rome. A short time afterwards, Melanchthon aided Luther in the conference at Marburg with Zwingli, appointed, by landgrave Philip of Hesse, for the purpose of effecting an agreement between the Lutherans and Zwinglians in regard to the doctrine of the Lord's Supper, which for some years had been the subject of a heated controversy. Luther contended that Christ's body is really present in the bread and wine of the Supper, "in, with, and under" the elements, maintaining what is known as the doctrine of "consubstantiation," as opposed to the Romish doctrine of "transubstantiation," which affirms the *change* of the bread and wine into the body and blood of Christ. Zwingli and his followers held the view that the bread and wine are signs of the Saviour's body and blood, and that the latter are to be partaken of by the soul alone, through faith. Each of the two parties based its view upon a different understanding of the word "is" in our Lord's declaration at the institution of the Supper: "This *is* my body . . . my blood," Luther taking it as literal; the Swiss party apprehending it as equivalent to *signifies*.

The conference at Marburg did not bring the parties to an agreement on the contested point. Neither would yield, for each firmly believed that its doctrine was taught in the Scriptures.

The imperial diet assembled at Augsburg in

May, 1530, and, after the arrival of the emperor later, was formally opened June 20th, with a statement of the subjects to be discussed—resistance to the Turks, and the religious disagreements. The Reformers were required to present their confession of faith before the assembly. This, the first Protestant confession, which is still the standard of belief in the Lutheran church, was drawn up chiefly by Melanchthon, who labored over it with prayers and tears. It had the approval of Luther, then at Coburg, and was signed by the Protestant princes and the representatives of most of the Protestant imperial cities. It was on the occasion of the signature of this document that the elector John of Saxony won his title of "the Steadfast," for avowing his determination to confess Christ at the hazard of any earthly loss, which, he said, could be but temporal, while his dependence upon his Saviour and Master was for eternity.

The confession was read in the imperial chapel of the bishop's palace, June 25th, and won the admiration of many of the multitude of listeners. It was then submitted to a committee of Romish theologians, for their refutation of it.

In the meantime, while the refutation was being prepared, means were taken to draw concessions from Melanchthon, who, for the love of peace, was at times disposed to concede more than he ought, though never enough to satisfy the desires of Rome. He became much dejected, and suffered in health; but Luther wrote to him encouraging words, enjoined firmness, and asked him, "What more can the devil do than to kill us? Why, then, be troubled?"

The refutation was read before the diet, August 3d, and the Protestants were required to own themselves convinced by it, and to abandon their errors. It was a violent but very weak defence of Romish doctrine, and Melanchthon ably refuted it in his reply, entitled "The Apology of the Augsburg Confession."

Repeated conferences and mutual concessions failed to effect any agreement between the Papists and the Protestants in regard to the disputed points, and the issue of the diet was a *recess* or decree forbidding the Protestants to make any efforts whatever to extend their faith, but granting them until the 15th of the following April to decide whether they would return to the Romish Church.

Early in the following year, 1531, the Protestant princes and cities entered into the League of Schmalkalden, for the purpose of defending the evangelical truth and its confessors by the sword, if necessary, against any violence on the part of their Romish opponents. In 1532, however, an agreement was arrived at, at the Diet of Nuremberg, proclaiming a peace between the two parties, and suspending all hostilities on either side, pending the meeting of a general council, or the issue of another imperial recess.

For several years the Reformation progressed, interrupted in some measure by the fanatical excesses of the Anabaptists, and answering persecutions on the part of the Romanists. Meantime, efforts were again made to secure an agreement between the Lutherans and the Zwinglians in regard to the Lord's Supper; and although neither party yielded its peculiar views, a friendly understanding was at length, 1536, established for a time, chiefly through the mediation of Bucer of Strasburg.

In 1537 Luther, at the elector John Frederick's request, drew up a confession to be laid before a general council convoked to meet at Mantua. This confession, entitled "Articles of Schmalkalden," from the place of its signature, during a Protestant conference held there, was bold in its denunciation of the pope, a circumstance which Melanchthon so much regretted as to append an additional article stating his own willingness to submit to the pope's supremacy, *as a human institution*, if the pope would not oppose the progress of the gospel.

The emperor was still exceedingly desirous of the establishment of harmony within his dominions, especially on account of the danger constantly threatening from the Turks, whom a divided empire could not quell. Thus the followers of the false prophet, in disposing Charles to conciliatory measures towards his Protestant subjects, were, in the admirable providence of God, repeatedly made subservient to the establishment of the pure faith of the gospel in Germany. Melanchthon was present, among other Protestant leaders, and popish representatives, at a meeting in the interests of peace held at Frankfort-on-the-Main, February, 1539, whose result was a fifteen months' truce. Similar assemblies were held at Hagenau, Worms, and Ratisbon, in 1540 and 1541. While Melanchthon was on his way to the first, he fell ill at Weimar, and Luther, who was sent for, found him apparently at the point of death. Distressed at the prospect of losing so valuable an ally in the defence of the gospel, Luther poured forth a most earnest prayer for his friend's recovery; and both he and Melanchthon believed that it was in answer to this prayer that the life of the latter was spared. At Ratisbon, Melanchthon was one of the three Protestant theologians selected by the emperor to confer with an equal number of Catholics, the result of whose joint deliberations was their partial adoption of the Ratisbon Interim, which expressed an agreement between the two bodies of theologians on certain points, but was satisfactory to neither Papists nor Protestants. Poor Melanchthon was blamed by the emperor for not having conceded enough, and censured by many of his friends for having yielded too much. He reproached himself afterwards for having made any concessions. In default of any better arrangement, the emperor renewed the peace of Nuremberg.

In 1545, Melanchthon, at his elector's request, drew up a new statement of the principles of the Reformers, for presentation at the diet held at Worms in that year. Early in the following year, he was called upon to assist at Luther's funeral.

After the war between the Protestant allies and the emperor had issued in the destruction of the Schmalkaldic League, and in the placing of Duke Maurice of Saxony in the electoral chair of his cousin John Frederick, against whom Maurice, though a Protestant, had, for political reasons, sided with the emperor, Charles still cherished the hope that further conferences might bring about a religious agreement. At the Diet of Augsburg held in July, 1547, two Catholic bishops, and the Protestant chaplain of the elector of Brandenburg, drew up an ecclesiastical constitution in which most important concessions were made to the Papists, in regard to justification by faith, the papacy, the intercession of saints, and the mass. This constitution was legalized by the emperor in the following year, and was what is known as the Second, or Augsburg Interim. It proved satisfactory to neither party, and was heartily opposed by the Protestants, many of their clergy preferring persecution and exile to compliance with its requisitions. Melanchthon was unusually bold in his opposition to it.

But Melanchthon gave great offence to many of the more uncompromising leaders — Calvin among others — by the part which he bore soon after, 1548, in the preparation, at the elector Maurice's request, of a third Interim, drawn up at a convention of Maurice's theologians at Leipsic. In this instrument, also, concessions were made to the Romanists, more particularly in liturgical observances, called *adiaphora*, or indifferent things. In the adiaphoristic controversy which followed, Melanchthon had to endure the harshest attacks, even from former pupils; while, at the same time, any manifestation on his part of reluctance to come to an agreement with the Romish Church exposed him to the charge of seditiousness. Yet, unwilling to leave Germany at so critical a time, Melanchthon refused to escape from his trying and painful position, though a call to England presented him with a favorable opportunity. Admirable, also, were the Christian gentleness and meekness with which he bore, and responded to, unmerciful attacks.

In March, 1552, the elector Maurice took up arms against the emperor in behalf of the Protestant cause. In his victorious march southward to Innsbruck, where Charles then was, he everywhere declared the Protestants released from obedience to the Augsburg interim, and reinstated Protestant magistrates and preachers. The emperor, obliged to flee by night from Innsbruck, and finding himself attacked at the same time by Maurice's ally, Henry II. of France, and also by the ever-troublesome Turks, empowered his brother Ferdinand to establish terms of peace with Maurice. The treaty of Passau, concluded at this time, August, 1552, guaranteed religious liberty to the Protestants; and although the imperial sanction of its provisions was deferred for a time, by dissensions among the Protestant leaders, the Diet of Augsburg, opened February 5, 1555, finally secured a permanent religious peace which gave to the Lutherans equal religious and political rights with the Catholics.

The disputes among the theologians still went on, Melanchthon continuing to take a leading part.

The synergistic controversy, and that with Osiander, concerning justification and sanctification, occupied most of his time; but he was ever ready to do what he could to forward the cause of union, not only among the Protestants, but also with the Romanists. For this purpose he attended a conference at Worms in 1557, but without any good results. The great doctrine of toleration was not yet fully accepted, and the whole church was in error respecting the authority of the civil magistrate in religious matters. In addition to Melanchthon's public trials and anxieties, he had also various domestic afflictions. One son died in childhood, and another gave his father much concern by his levity. His daughter Anna was unhappily married, and died before Melanchthon. The loss of his wife occurred in 1557, and his own health began seriously to decline in 1558. The end of his labors and disputations was now near; and Melanchthon, worn by the incessant toils and conflicts of the stormy age in which he lived, thought joyfully of his approaching deliverance from sin and the rancor of theological dispute, and his admission to the visible presence of his God and Saviour, and to a more extended knowledge of the mysteries of redemption.

In March, 1560, he departed for Leipsic on business of the elector, and returned from this journey stricken with his last sickness. On the 19th of April he was released from his labors, and taken home to his heavenly rest. As he neared the end of his pilgrimage, his son-in-law, Dr. Peucer asked him if he wished for anything, to which he replied, "Nothing but heaven."

Thus died one of the ablest and noblest men of the Reformation. Too timid to be just such a leader as Luther, at the same time he possessed the qualifications which were necessary to make Luther's more efficient. Luther could not have performed Melanchthon's scholarly work, any more than Melanchthon could have accomplished Luther's pioneer work. Melanchthon was the systemizer of the faith of the church of the Reformation in Germany; and his spirit of moderation has, with beneficial effects, been transmitted to the present day.

He was buried, as we have already described, in his beloved Wittenberg, and in 1869 a monument was completed to his memory.

ULRIC ZWINGLI.

On October 12th, 1531, nearly sixteen years before the death of Luther, and the same year in which the League of Schmalkalden was formed, there lay, fearfully wounded, on the battlefield of Cappel, one of Switzerland's greatest men, one of her greatest reformers, preachers, and statesmen. As the blood trickled from his wounds, he exclaimed, "What matters this misfortune? they may, indeed, kill the body, but they cannot kill the soul." Let us note a few of the incidents in this man's life, and the cause of his being on this battlefield.

Seven weeks after the birth of Luther, Ulric Zwingli was born, January 1, 1484, in a little cottage in the mountain village of Wildhaus, some twenty miles east of the lake of Zurich. His father was a shepherd, and also bailiff of Wildhaus, the Zwinglis being highly esteemed in all the country round. Ulric was the third of eight sons, who, with one daughter, comprised the family of the bailiff. The love of country was early aroused in the boy's heart by the stories of Swiss patriotism related in his hearing by his father and others; and a religious feeling was, at the same time, excited by stories from the Bible, and the legends of the church, told him by his mother and grandmother.

His father's brother Bartholomew was dean of Wesen, and to him Ulric was early entrusted, in the hope that he might be fitted for something higher than a shepherd's life on his native mountains. The dean soon became very fond of the boy, and interested himself heartily in his education. When Ulric was only ten years old, he showed signs of such mental superiority that he was sent to Basel; and on learning all that he could acquire at the elementary school there, he was removed to Berne, where he enjoyed the instructions of Wölflin, or Lupulus, a distinguished scholar and poet of the day. There Ulric made such progress in classical learning that the Dominican monks, attracted by his talents and his fine voice, desired him to enter their order. To prevent this, his father and uncle transferred him to Vienna, where he began the study of scholastic philosophy. After leaving Vienna and spending a short time at home, Ulric in 1502 returned to Basel, to teach school, and at the same time pursue his own studies in philosophy and theology at the university, where he was graduated as Master of Arts. There he came under the influence of the learned and pious theologian Thomas Wyttenbach, who made the Scriptures the chief source of his instructions, and taught that "the death of Christ is the only ransom of our souls."

In 1506, Zwingli, then twenty-two, was invited to become pastor of Glarus. He was accordingly ordained, and removed to his large parish, after reading his first mass at Wildhaus.

The state of religion at the time when he began the work of his pastorate may easily be learned from the fact, that in a synod which assembled early in the sixteenth century, only three of its members had read the Bible; the others confessed that they had hardly any knowledge of the New Testament. They contented themselves with repeating sermons which were prepared by the monks, and which were often wholly unsuited to the circumstances of the congregation. But Zwingli was a man of a different type. He had a desire for information, and sought even among the writings of Wickliffe and Huss to obtain it, though then without any purpose of accepting their doctrines. During his ten years' pastorate at Glarus, he did not attack the errors of Rome, but strove to reform the morals and politics of his people. Besides discharging his ordinary pastoral duties with unusual fidelity and purity of life, Zwingli gave much time to study of the classics and the Scriptures. Being very poor, he would have found it difficult to procure books, had it not been for a pension of fifty florins bestowed upon him by the pope, because of the favorable representations of Cardinal Schinner, bishop of Sitten and papal legate, who was struck with Zwingli's talent and influence, and desired his attachment to the papal interests.

Twice, in 1512 and 1515, Zwingli, at the order of his government, accompanied the troops of Glarus to Italy, whither they were summoned to take part in the engagements between the pope and his allies, and the French. For upwards of sixty years the Swiss had been in the habit of selling their military services to foreign powers. Zwingli, who saw the evil effects of this mercenary service upon the character of his countrymen, in promoting avarice, luxury, and immorality, denounced the practice in the strongest terms, in his sermons and in published writings.

In a letter to the canton of Schweitz, he says: "Think how many of your fellow-citizens have perished in the wars of Naples, in the battles of Navarre and Milan. What rivers of blood have you not shed! What would you say if you were to see the mercenary soldier, hired with gold—whom you had never injured—appearing at your gates, felling your woods, destroying your vines, carrying off your flocks, massacring your children, unaffected by the tears of your wives and your fathers, butchering them before your own eyes, and setting fire to your dwellings? Yet this is what you yourselves do, allured by the charm of riches and property unjustly acquired."

During Zwingli's later years at Glarus, the study of the New Testament in the original Greek engaged much of his attention. He committed large portions of it to memory, earnestly praying that the Holy Spirit would cause him to understand it — a prayer which was abundantly answered; and he laid its truths, as he discovered them, before his people.

In 1514 he made the acquaintance of Erasmus, then on a visit to Basel, to which city Zwingli journeyed for the sake of seeing and speaking with a man whose writings he had long admired. In this visit to Basel he was thrown into the society of other men of genius and learning assembled around Erasmus.

Zwingli was called to Einsiedeln, in Schweitz, in 1516; and, notwithstanding the protests of the people of Glarus, he accepted the appointment as affording him a larger field of usefulness. He was, also, partly influenced by the ascendancy gained in Glarus by the French party won by the persuasions and bribes of Francis I., who now desired Swiss aid against the emperor and the pope.

Einsiedeln was the seat of a monastery dedicated to the Virgin, to which large crowds of pilgrims flocked, attracted by the fame of an image reputed to work miracles, by the offer of "complete remission of sins," in an inscription over the gate of the abbey, and by the yearly commemoration of the alleged consecration of the abbey-church by Christ and angels. The retirement of a residence in the abbey gave Zwingli more leisure to pursue his study of the Word of God, love for which was continually increasing in his heart, while he endeavored more and more to conform his life to its precepts. Here he gained a nearer view of the superstitions and corruptions of the Romish church. And here, with the numerous and ever-changing throngs of misled pilgrims as his auditors, he faithfully and impressively preached salvation by Christ alone. When accused, years later, of being a Lutheran, he declared that he had "learned the doctrine of Christ from God's Word," and preached it, before Luther's name was heard in Switzerland.

Zwingli formed several valued and helpful friendships at Einsiedeln, and it was doubtless owing to his influence that the administrator of the abbey caused the inscription over its gate to be removed. To Schinner and the other papal legates who visited Einsiedeln, and who sought by promises and favors to secure Zwingli's political influence to the pope, he boldly expressed his sense of the corruptions of the church, and his intention to proclaim the truth as he found it in the Scriptures. In the summer of 1518 he denounced the indulgence-seller Samson, then pursuing his trade in the Swiss cantons, and prevented him from reaping much profit in Schweitz.

Zwingli's reputation as a preacher was now very great, and, owing partly to the exertions of his friend Oswald Myconius, he was invited to fill the important charge of preacher and pastor in the cathedral of Zurich. He preached his first sermon there on Saturday, January 1, 1519.

"An immense audience was assembled, and he commenced by showing that Christ is the sole author of salvation, and the only hope and consolation of sinners. He then proceeded to inveigh against vice in general, and particularly hypocrisy, recommended works of piety, and thundered against luxury, idleness, and intemperance."

On the following day he began a course of sermons on the Gospel of Matthew, declaring that the life of Jesus had been too long neglected; and on week-days he lectured on the Old Testament.

Multitudes of every class thronged to hear him, and many were led by him to the one true source of salvation. He was equally faithful in his pastoral visitations, and also continued to pursue his studies diligently, devoting a good portion of his time to Hebrew, that he might better understand the mind of the Spirit as revealed in the Old Testament. When Samson approached the city of Zurich, Zwingli influenced the council and the townspeople against his indulgences, and the sale of his wares in the canton was forbidden.

In the summer of 1519 Zwingli's health became impaired by his exertions, and he went to the baths of Pfeffers. But, hearing while there that the plague had broken out in Zurich, he immediately returned to his post, and, while laboring among his stricken parishioners, was himself smitten down by the dread disease. On his unexpected recovery great was the joy of his family and his friends, among whom a report of his death had spread. Upon himself his illness had the effect of increasing his devotion to his Saviour, and his ability to minister for him at whose feet he had thrown himself in more simple faith, and in utter hopelessness of all other help, during the dark time of bodily pain, and of spiritual depression in view of sin and the apparent closeness of eternity. Unmoved by the flattery and offered bribes of papal nuncios, he henceforth more fervently preached the infinite value of Christ's obedience and death as the sinner's Substitute, and the power of his love to win the soul to a life of loving obedience to him. "Only love to the Redeemer," he declared, "could impel man to the performance of actions acceptable to God;" and he urged his hearers to see to it that Christ was in them, and that they were in Christ. Not only the people of Zurich, who crowded to the cathedral, heard these words, but many strangers from all parts of the confederacy were among Zwingli's auditors from time to time; and thus the truth spread through Switzerland, as it was spreading through Germany.

At about this time the canons of the cathedral, uneasy at Zwingli's course because it tended to diminish their influence and their revenues, began seriously to oppose him. Their opposition did not, however, prevent the Council of Zurich in 1520 from ordering all preachers to found their sermons on the Word of God alone. But this civil mandate drew forth the condemnation of the bishop of Constance, in whose diocese Zurich was, and greatly offended many monks who were ignorant of the Bible.

Some of Zwingli's adherents having ceased to observe the appointed fasts, and also tried to force others to follow them, the council requested Zwingli to instruct the people on this point in his sermons. Besides doing this, Zwingli published a tract on the subject, in which, with apostolic moderation, he urged that true Christian liberty did not consist in claiming the right to eat meat; and when cited to appear before the council and a deputation from the bishop, he proposed that fasting should be continued for the present. In the spring of 1522 Zwingli and his clerical associates in the furtherance of the gospel introduced some important changes in the church services, substituting a German liturgy in the place of the Latin one, and dropping some useless and superstitious ceremonies in baptism. Soon after the bishop of Constance wrote to the council and clergy of Zurich concerning the innovations of Zwingli as follows:

"Do not," said he, "allow them to be preached among you, nor discussed publicly or privately; preserve yourselves in the doctrines and usages of the church, till those to whom it belongs shall regulate these matters."

In reply, Zwingli and several of his friends addressed letters to the bishop and to the whole confederation, petitioning that the gospel might be freely preached in the cantons, and that unscriptural regulations might be abolished.

In the meantime the Council of Worms, 1521, had proscribed Luther. Now Zwingli was charged with being a Lutheran, and a violent controversy arose between the opposed parties.

Plots were laid against Zwingli's life, and the council deemed it necessary to guard his house. To settle the dispute, if possible, Zwingli solicited a conference, and the state authorities provided for one, January 29, 1523. Zwingli propounded sixty-seven propositions which he wished discussed, and took the precaution to circulate them among the people before the conference assembled. Among other things, he affirmed that "the gospel is the only rule of faith; that Christ is the only Head of the church; that traditions are to be rejected; that the mass is not a sacrifice; that the priests have a right to marry," etc.

The conference met, but the representatives of Rome, true to their history, refused, for some time, to discuss; and little was accomplished, except that the council resolved "that Zwingli, having neither been convicted of heresy, nor refuted from the Scriptures, should continue to preach the gospel as he had done hitherto; that the pastors of Zurich and its territory should rest their discourses on the words of Scripture alone, and that both parties should refrain from all personal reflections."

Zwingli desired the abolition of the mass and of images. Some iconoclastic proceedings on the part of a few violent persons in Zurich made urgent the need for a decision in regard to images; and, accordingly, a second conference was held on two successive days of October, 1523, in the presence of nine hundred persons; including the council, three hundred and fifty priests from different parts of the canton of Zurich, and representatives from Schaffhausen and St. Gall. The other cantons, as well as the bishops of Constance, Chur, and Basel, declined Zurich's invitation to send deputies. The result was a complete victory for the Reformers, the adoration of images and the Romish mass being proved to be contrary to the Scriptures. In the following year the council ordered the daily preaching of the Word of God, and the abolition of images and of all unscriptural practices in the celebration of the mass, measures which were orderly carried out, in spite of another protest from the bishop of Constance. Pilgrimages were abolished about the same time. A further change, effected in April, 1525, was the administration of the Lord's supper to the people in a perfectly simple form, disencumbered of all the ceremonies of the mass.

In April, 1524, Zwingli, like Luther a year later, began a happy home-life for himself by his marriage with Anna Reinhart, the widow of a distinguished magistrate.

One measure of importance in which Zwingli was at this period actively interested, was the establishment of an academic and theological school on the foundation of the cathedral-chapter, the majority of the canons having been converted to Zwingli's views and become inspired with the desire for a life of greater activity and usefulness. Zwingli, beside his other labors, discharged the duties of professor of theology.

In Berne, where the gospel had at first been preached amid many discouragements by Berthold Haller, the friends of the Reformation had become numerous, and a discussion was appointed to take place between them and the adherents of Rome in the beginning of 1528. Zwingli was one of the three hundred and fifty clergymen who attended the conference, which resulted in the triumph of the evangelical party, and, later, in the establishment, by the council, of regulations in regard to doctrine and worship like those which prevailed at Zurich. A further result was the conclusion, in June, 1528, of an offensive and defensive alliance between Zurich and Berne. Constance was already allied with Zurich, and the confederation was afterwards joined by St. Gall, Basel, Biel, and Mülhausen. Opposed to this evangelical alliance was a Romanist league, comprising the five cantons of Uri, Schweitz, Unterwalden, Zug, and Lucerne.

The persecutions and martyrdom inflicted by the Romish cantons upon a number of confessors of the Reformed faith enraged the Protestant cantons and cities, and caused a portion of the evangelical believers to look to the sword as the proper means of settling the conflict of opinions. Prominent among the advocates of war was Zwingli. He armed himself and accompanied the troops of Zurich to the field in the summer of 1529, when the cutting off of supplies on both sides had been followed by the muster of armies and preparations for an encounter. War was avoided for a time by the exertions of a peace-party, who concluded a treaty of peace at Steinhausen, in Zug, July 26, 1529.

Soon after, Zwingli repaired to the conference at Marburg. He had become involved in the sacramental controversy with Luther in 1527, and conducted his part of it with great moderation and forbearance. At the conclusion of the conference, articles setting forth the points on which the two parties agreed were signed.

But troubles awaited Zwingli on his return from Marburg. The peace which had been agreed upon at Steinhausen was disregarded by the Romish cantons, and the professors of the Reformed religion in those cantons were again persecuted. Even in Zurich enemies of the gospel gained some ground, and Zwingli, in discouragement, offered his resignation, which, however, was declined.

In July, 1530, Zwingli transmitted a confession of faith to the emperor, then at the Diet of Augsburg, before which the Lutheran confession was laid. In almost all important points the two confessions were in harmony.

The disagreements between the Reformed and the Romish cantons advanced speedily to an open rupture, both parties transgressing the terms of peace. While Zwingli still counselled war, and was confident of the ultimate triumph of the pure faith, sad forebodings of the trials awaiting the church in the near future filled his mind, and, in accordance with the superstitious view of the age, he regarded the great comet of 1531 as a portent of such troubles.

When the Protestant cantons hindered the passage of supplies for the Romish cantons, the latter determined upon immediate warfare. On October 9, 1531, the five popish cantons took the field, moving an army of eight thousand men towards the city of Zurich. The people of Zurich, taken by surprise, sent out an advance-guard, consisting of but nineteen hundred men, who met the enemy's forces at Cappel. Zwingli, who appeared to have a presentiment that he would never return to his home, accompanied the Zurichers into the very thickest of the battle; and while he was administering the consolations of religion to a dying soldier he was himself struck down by one of the stones used in the fight according to ancient Swiss custom. He rose, but was thrice more felled to the ground, the last time by a lance-thrust, when he uttered the words recorded in the beginning of our sketch. Catholic soldiers found him later, and, not recognizing him in the darkness, urged him to pray to the Virgin and the saints. Infuriated by his silent refusal, they turned his face towards the light of a fire. One of their captains happened to pass as they uttered their suspicion that it was Zwingli on whom they were gazing, and he gave the reformer his death-stroke. For Zwingli, mistaken as he doubtless was in advocating and grasping the sword as a defence of the gospel, the blow which despatched him was really a "stroke of mercy," sending him to the presence of that divine Saviour upon whom he had long personally relied, and whom he had faithfully set forth as the only way of salvation.

The most violent of his enemies were not satisfied with his death. His body was condemned on the next day as that of a traitor and heretic; it was accordingly quartered and burned, the ashes were mingled with the ashes of swine, and scattered to the winds.

Six hundred brave Zurichers fell with Zwingli, and great was the lamentation in the city of the slain, and elsewhere, for the grief and loss that had come upon the cause of the Reformed. One of the greatest sufferers was Zwingli's widow, who at Cappel lost husband, son, son-in-law, brother, and brother-in-law.

But though Zwingli was dead, his work remained. It needed to be purified with fire, and it was; but by-and-by it shone forth in beauty and strength. Being thus early taken away from his work before it was fully established, he acquired less celebrity than either Luther, Calvin, or Knox; but he was not a whit behind them in his love for the truth and in his ability to distinguish it from error. He had remarkably clear views of Scripture truth, and courage to maintain them. To remotest times he will be remembered as one of the greatest men of Switzerland, and one of the clearest-headed of the reformers of the sixteenth century.

JOHN CALVIN.

In the cemetery of Plain-Palais, outside the city of Geneva, on the banks of the Rhone, a plain stone may be seen with the letters J. C. chiselled upon it. Guides point it out as marking the last resting-place of the famous theologian and reformer, John Calvin. But it is a matter of little moment that the place of his sepulchre is scarcely known, and that no costly monument marks his grave. The influences which he set in motion for civil and religious liberty, for right, truth, and humanity, for the glory of God and the good of men, are still pervading the world, and form a nobler monument than any that the hands of his friends could have erected. It is emphatically true of him that, "though dead, he yet speaks."

Calvin was born at Noyon, in Picardy, France, July 10, 1509, nearly one hundred years later than John Huss, and almost thirty years later than Luther. His father, Gerard Calvin, was a very intelligent man, and discharged several important civil and ecclesiastical offices for the county and diocese of Noyon. At his own expense he had John, his second son, educated in the household of the De Montmors, a noble family of the neighborhood. When the boy was twelve years old, his father, who perceived his talents and wished to fit him for the priesthood, induced the bishop of Noyon to appoint him chaplain of the little chapel of Notre Dame de la Gesine; and John accordingly received the tonsure, and was installed May 29, 1521. About two years afterwards the plague broke out at Noyon, and John, aided by the salary of his chaplaincy, accompanied the young De Montmors to Paris. There he studied the Latin classics in the College de la Marche, and applied himself to dialectics and scholastic philosophy in the College Montaign, outstripping his fellow-students at both institutions, and gaining by his own strict morality and his frank disapprobation of wrong-doing on the part of others the nickname of "the Accusative."

Though it does not appear that he was at any time formally ordained, in his nineteenth year he was advanced to another benefice, which he exchanged nearly two years later, July, 1529, for the curacy of Pont l'Evêque, a village near Noyon, where he preached. At about this time his father, perceiving that the calling which he had chosen for his son was not a very lucrative one, endeavored to turn his attention to the study of law. The proposed change was not unacceptable to the young man, as he had already begun to doubt some of the doctrines of the church, influenced by the study of the Bible, to which he had been led by his relative Pierre Robert Olivetan, reviser of Lefêvre's French translation of the Scriptures.

At Orleans, where Calvin began his legal studies under the celebrated Professor Pierre de l'Étoile, he was, as he tells us, "suddenly converted," and filled with an earnest desire to learn and do the will of God. He applied himself to the study of law with an assiduity and success which enabled him to fill the place of the professor when the latter was absent, and procured him, on his departure from the college, the title of *doctor* without payment of the customary fees. Theology also engaged Calvin's attention at Orleans, and had for him a greater attraction than law. At the college of Bourges, where his legal education was continued under Alciati, a learned Italian professor, Melchior Volmar, a Swabian, was professor of Greek. Calvin studied Greek and the New Testament under him, and by conversation with him was confirmed in adherence to the principles of the Reformation. He had already joined the company of evangelical believers at Orleans; and at Bourges he was impelled by a sense of duty, contrary to his natural inclination for retirement, to teach privately and publicly the doctrines which he had embraced. Young as he was, many sought his instruction and advice; and he preached to the poor and the rich in the neighboring hamlets and mansions.

After his father's death Calvin resided for two years at Noyon. In 1529 he went to Paris, where he lived with Étienne de la Forge, aftewards a martyr to the Reformed faith. In the house of this man Calvin often preached to assemblies of believers, whom, in the midst of actual and threatening persecutions, he encouraged to trust and fidelity. Finally, to the joy of his friends, he abandoned the study of law and devoted himself wholly to theology; and in 1532, although in need of money, he resigned his benefices, which he could no longer conscientiously hold. Already he was regarded as the leader of the Reformed movement in France, a movement which the Sorbonne, the leading theological college of the university of Paris, had condemned as heretical, and which Francis I. was endeavoring to crush with a violence that had sent many into exile or prison, and several to the stake. It was under such circumstances that Calvin composed for his friend Nicholas Cop, new rector of the Sorbonne, an address which boldly defended the proscribed evangelical doctrines, and especially that of justification by faith alone. This address, delivered by Cop at his inauguration on the feast of All-Saints, 1533, so aroused the indignation of the king, the parliament, and the Sorbonne, that both the speaker and the writer were obliged to seek safety in flight.

At Saintonge, in the home of Louis du Tillet, a canon of Angoulême, and at Nérac, the residence of the king's sister, Queen Margaret of Navarre, who was herself an earnest disciple of the Reformed faith, Calvin, under the name of d'Espeville, found a temporary refuge. At the queen's court he made the acquaintance of Lefêvre, who had boldly proclaimed the truths of the gospel from his chair in the Sorbonne, and banished thence, was now the tutor of Queen Margaret's children.

In 1534 Calvin returned to Paris, where, however, he lived in concealment, until, "at no small risk to his life," as he says, he came forth from his seclusion to engage in a theological discussion with Servetus, who was already proclaiming his peculiar opinions: but the Spaniard, less fearless than Calvin, failed to appear.

Persecution again drove Calvin from Paris and from France. After stopping for a while at Poitiers, where, in a grotto outside of the town, he celebrated the Lord's supper with a large company of the Reformed who had gathered round him for instruction; and at Orleans, where he published a treatise against the Anabaptists' theory that the soul sleeps after death, he went, with Du Tillet, to Strasburg, and was warmly welcomed by Bucer. He next repaired to Basel, where he studied Hebrew under Capito, the leader of the Reformation there. At Basel, in 1536, Calvin published, in Latin, his work on the "Institutes of the Christian Religion," which he had hastily prepared in defence of the faith of the Reformed, who were accused of holding Anabaptist tenets and wishing to subvert all civil authority. As Francis I. helped to circulate this calumny, declaring, through his ambassadors to the German Protestant princes, whose friendship he desired to retain, that the punishments inflicted upon "Lutheran heretics" in his own dominions were justified by the evil opinions and character of the sufferers, Calvin dedicated his book to the king, and addressed him in a forcible preface, defending the Protestants, and exposing the false claims of Rome. The body of the work consisted of treatises on the Ten Commandments, the Apostles' Creed, the Lord's Prayer, and the sacraments, on Christian liberty, the false sacraments of Rome, and the authority and polity of the church of Christ. Calvin insisted strongly on the sinful corruption of the whole nature of man consequent on the fall of Adam and transmitted to all his descendants, by reason of which original corruption each individual merits the wrath and punishment of God; upon the inability of man to deliver himself from this state of guilt and sin; and upon the sovereignty of God, as shown in the grace by which, through the operation of the Holy Spirit, he inclines to himself those whom he has chosen to save through Christ.

This work—which excelled any system of theology before prepared, and which, though the author was but twenty-six when it was published, was composed with such maturity of thought and judgment that it was afterwards subjected to elaboration only, not change—became very popular. Calvin soon translated it into French, and from time to time, as successive editions were required, revised and enlarged it. Its influence has been immense on religious thought and practice and ecclesiastical government from Calvin's own time to the present day, and it is still a theological "classic."

From Basel Calvin went to the court of Renée, daughter of Louis XII. of France, and wife of the Duke of Ferrara. She, like the Queen of Navarre, was a disciple of the Reformers, and near her Calvin, again under the assumed name of

Charles d'Espeville, found an asylum for a time: but his conversation, his sermons, and his life, soon drew upon him the attention of the agents of the Inquisition, and it became necessary for him to leave Italy.

After some further wanderings he arrived, in August, 1536, at Geneva, where he met his old friend and protector, Louis du Tillet, who introduced him to Farel, at that time the leading Protestant minister in Geneva. Calvin had no thought of remaining in this city, which he had visited on his way to Basel, where he intended to settle and devote himself to study, but Farel knew that he was the very man needed in Geneva at that formative period of the Reformation, and determined that he would not permit him to leave. The discussion which ensued between these noble men, as detailed by the historian of the Reformation, is very remarkable. No doubt Farel was, as Calvin finally believed, impressed by the Spirit of God to urge the other to undertake the work in Geneva. Calvin trembled under the zealous words of Farel: "May God curse your repose, may God curse your studies, if, in such a great necessity as ours, you withdraw, and refuse to give us your help." Calvin yielded, and began the work of lecturing on theology, and afterwards of preaching, being appointed pastor of the cathedral of St. Peter.

Geneva was just then at a critical period. It had lately (1526) thrown off the rule of the dukes of Savoy, and established a republican government, in alliance with Berne and Freiburg. Farel, Froment, and other evangelical preachers, had proclaimed the gospel there, and won adherents, in spite of the opposition of a determined and powerful Romish party. Protestant Berne, by virtue of its alliance with Geneva, insisted that the Genevese should be permitted to choose between the gospel and the pope. In July, 1533, the bishop withdrew from the stormy scenes in the city. After two public disputations (1534) between Romanists and Reformers, when the latter were victorious, and a series of struggles in which blood flowed on both sides, allegiance to the bishop was finally renounced, and the Council of Geneva, in August, 1535, abolished the Romish rites and legalized evangelical preaching and worship.

But the Reformation was only begun. Many of the popish doctrines were still cherished, and the Genevese, from their imperfect enlightenment, were in danger of being led into error by fanatical teachers, such as the Anabaptists. One of the first acts of Calvin, together with Farel, was the preparation of a brief system of Christian doctrine, which the citizens of Geneva were required to profess and swear to. The secular and religious education of children was provided for by the establishment of schools, in which a catechism prepared by Calvin formed one of the studies. The Anabaptists were finally silenced in a disputation in March, 1537. This, however, was only the beginning of a succession of struggles for Calvin. He and Farel were accused of holding wrong views in regard to the Trinity; but their belief was vindicated, and their defamer, Peter Caroli, a reformed pastor of Lausanne, was banished. Dissensions next arose in Geneva about the strict ecclesiastical discipline which Calvin and his colleagues in the ministry were endeavoring to enforce, the simplicity of the ritual which Farel had introduced, and the Reformers' determined resistance to dictation from the government in regard to usages of worship, preaching, and other church matters. At Easter, 1538, so violent was the popular rage against the preachers that Calvin and Farel refused to celebrate the Lord's supper, on the ground that the people were unfit for it. This action was followed by the pastors' banishment from Geneva, and the government and people refused to receive them back even when the synod of the Swiss clergy requested that they might be allowed to return.

Calvin next settled at Strasburg, where he was pastor of a congregation of about 1,500 French refugees, and also lectured on theology. There he prepared a new edition of his *Institutes*, wrote a commentary on *Romans* and a treatise on the Lord's supper — books which gave Luther lively satisfaction—and revised Olivetan's French Bible. In 1540 he married Idelette de Bures, widow of an Anabaptist whom Calvin had converted. Until 1549, when she died, to the great and lasting grief of her husband, Calvin found her, as he says, "a precious help" who "never opposed him." In 1541 he made the acquaintance of Melanchthon at the Diet of Ratisbon, and from "the teacher of Germany" received the title of "the theologian." His after relations with Melanchthon were most affectionate.

With Geneva Calvin kept up some connection by writing letters of judicious advice to those who were friendly to him there, and whose party—the Guillermins, or Williamites, from William Farel — gradually gained the ascendency over his opposers. When, in 1539, Cardinal Sadolet, taking advantage of the disorder and irreligion prevalent in Geneva, tried to win the Genevese back to the church of Rome, the task of answering his letter was committed to Calvin, and he ably refuted the cardinal's brilliant, but unsound arguments. The influential portion of the Genevese perceived that their city needed Calvin, and in 1540 the council sent him an urgent invitation to return. He declined it, but was finally prevailed upon to reënter the city as pastor and professor of theology, September 13, 1541, to the manifest joy of the people.

As Calvin had stipulated, his system of ecclesiastical government and discipline was adopted by the Genevese. The presbyterial system was inaugurated in a consistory composed of six ministers and twelve annually elected lay elders, who together formed a tribunal which met weekly for the consideration of cases of discipline, and possessed the power to inflict excommunication. The civil government was expected to follow up this decree with further penalties, when such were deemed necessary. Although offences which we should regard as trivial were often severely censured or punished, the effect of the system, conjoined with the public and private instruction in religion and morals arranged for by Calvin, was so conducive to the good order of the city that John Knox, who repeatedly visited it between 1554 and 1556, pronounced it "the most perfect school of Christ since the days of the apostles."

Calvin's labors were manifold and severe. He lectured on theology three days in the week, preached every day in every other week, met the consistory weekly, and read and expounded the Scriptures every Friday in the general meeting called the "congregation." Beside these duties, he was engaged in controversy on a variety of subjects, carried on an extensive correspondence, being appealed to from all quarters for advice, and wrote valuable Latin or French commentaries on almost all the books of the Bible. Soon after his return he was appointed one of a committee to codify the state laws of Geneva. He interested himself in the material prosperity of the city, revived its manufactures of cloth and velvet, and its trade in those articles, and introduced admirable sanitary regulations. Often, as he said, he had no time to look up at the sun or to sleep. Two thousand manuscript sermons of his are now in the library of Geneva.

A party—the Libertines—opposed to Calvin's theocratic ideas and ecclesiastical discipline was not lacking during his second residence in Geneva; and more than once he was called a second pope, and even threatened with death. Passing by his controversy with the Romanist Pighius, who opposed Calvin's presentation of the doctrine of predestination and election, but was converted to his antagonist's views, 1543, and the lengthier and more vexatious controversy on the same subject, in 1551, with Bolsec, formerly a Carmelite monk, which resulted in the banishment of Calvin's opponent for pertinacious maintenance of heresy, we must give some little notice to the trial of Servetus, Calvin's former challenger to a disputation in Paris.

Servetus made his appearance in Geneva in 1553, contrary to Calvin's expressed desire. He was accused by Calvin of heresy, chiefly in regard to the person of Christ, whom he regarded as in a sense divine, yet not the incarnate eternal Son of the Father. Servetus was arrested and imprisoned, tried before two of the three councils of Geneva, and condemned to be burned, together with the two books in which he had advocated his doctrines. Refusing to recant, his sentence was executed at Champel, about a mile from Geneva, October 27, 1553.

Calvin has been fiercely censured for his part in this matter. And, truly, the execution of Servetus was in accord with the spirit of Rome, papal and pagan, or the abrogated Old Testament laws of the Hebrew theocracy, rather than with the New Testament dispensation, and the mind of Him who rebuked his disciples for desiring to call down fire on a village that would not receive him. But it must be remembered that Calvin was far from originating capital punishment for heretical doctrine: it was the heritage from Rome of the Reformers in the age in which he lived. It was not the desire of Calvin that Servetus should be *burned;* he tried, in vain, to obtain the commutation of his sentence to beheading.

The execution of Servetus inflamed the enmity of Calvin's opponents in Geneva, and for several years he was involved in serious conflicts with the Libertines. The government sometimes opposed him, and sometimes supported him; and finally he saw his ecclesiastical system firmly established in Geneva, and imitated in other parts of Switzerland, and also in France and Scotland. Owing to his exertions, the new Academy of Geneva was opened in 1559, with Calvin's warm friend and biographer, Beza, as its first rector, and a list of six hundred students.

Calvin's unremitting labors favored the inroads of a variety of distressing diseases, which he suffered from for many years, but bravely battled against or disregarded, hating nothing so much as idleness. On February 6, 1564, he preached, with difficulty, his last sermon. After that he left his house but a few times, when he was carried on a litter to the council-hall and the church. Once a deputation from the council visited him on his sick-bed, and received his exhortation to use their authority to the glory of God. And several times the clergy of the city and neighborhood gathered around him. In the midst of intense sufferings his spirit was calm and peaceful, and he occupied himself with the Bible and in prayer. When Farel, in his eightieth year, heard of his sickness, he wrote from Neüfchatel that he would visit him, to which Calvin replied, in a letter dated May 2: "Farewell, my best and most right-hearted brother, and since God is pleased that you should survive me in this world, live mindful of our friendship, of which, as it was useful to the church of God, the fruit still awaits us in heaven. I would not have you fatigue yourself on my account. I draw my breath with difficulty, and am daily waiting till I altogether cease to breathe. It is enough that to Christ I live and die; to his people he is gain in life and death. Farewell again, not forgetting the brethren." Such words show that love as well as zeal had a place in Calvin's heart.

On the 27th of May, as the sun was setting, he fell asleep in Jesus. He was buried, as we have already stated, on the banks of the Rhone, outside of the city where he had so long labored in behalf of the religion of the Lord Jesus Christ. He asked that no monument might be placed upon his grave; and the spot where, some thirty years ago, the black stone was erected, is only conjectured to be his burial-place.

Prof. Tulloch well says of Calvin: "He was a great, intense, and energetic character, who more than any other even of that great age has left his impress on the history of Protestantism."

His clear intellect, and his logical acumen, together with his concise and crisp diction, make his works, even in the present day, a power in the church of God. He was needed in the church just as truly as Luther, Knox, or Wesley, and we thank God for the gift of such a man.

JOHN KNOX.

On the 26th day of November, 1572, in the presence of a large concourse of people, composed largely of the notable men of Scotland, Earl Morton, the regent of the kingdom, standing over an open grave in the churchyard of St. Giles, Edinburgh, pronounced this eulogy: "There lies he who never feared the face of man." The extraordinary man who called forth this eulogy was John Knox, and his life will form the subject of our present sketch.

He was born in 1505, at Giffordgate, a suburb of Haddington, in East-Lothian, Scotland, and was educated principally at the grammar-school of Haddington, and in the university of Glasgow. At the latter place he studied theology and philosophy under Prof. Mair, a man noted as being "an advanced thinker" at the time; and yet, judging by the writings he left, many of his discussions, says Dr. McCrie, were "utterly useless and trifling." Nevertheless, it is believed that both John Knox and George Buchanan, the celebrated scholar and historian, were largely influenced by him to pursue in an independent manner the investigation of the subjects that might come before them. At any rate, it is certain that both these pupils became leaders of thought, and their names yet live, an honor to their country.

For some unknown reason, Knox did not fit himself to receive the degree of master of arts at the university, and the course of his life for some years after he left there is uncertain. Without the degree of master he could not have been a regent or professor in any university, as he is sometimes, without proof, said to have been; but he may have taught privately. He was probably ordained a priest about 1530, and officiated for a number of years at or near Haddington.

At this period the Romish hierarchy controlled the whole country, and possessed a large share of its wealth. Bishops and abbots were privy councillors, and appointments to these positions were contended for with the same zeal and the same arts that wicked men employed to obtain secular positions. Inquiry was branded as infidelity; and learning, as the propagation of heresy. But though, in 1525, the Scottish parliament had passed a law prohibiting the importation of any of Luther's writings, or the immigration of any of his followers into Scotland, which had hitherto, says the act, "bene clene of all sic filth and vice," some of these writings found their way into the country, and thoughtful, independent men like Knox were prepared to read them.

Knox's attachment to the Romish church was shaken as early as 1535; and in 1542 he began to make his new faith and principles publicly known. As this conduct drew suspicion and enmity upon him, he withdrew from the diocese of St. Andrews, presided over by the persecuting archbishop and cardinal, Beaton, and went to the south of Scotland, where he aided George Wishart in the proclamation of those principles for which, in 1528, Patrick Hamilton had died. He carried before Wishart "a two-handed sword" as a token that he would defend him while he was preaching the gospel against any outbreak by lawless men. Wishart was, however, soon arrested by the authorities, and when Knox, who had already been declared a heretic and degraded from the priesthood, professed his readiness to stand by him, he repelled the offer, saying, "Return to your bairns; one is sufficient for a sacrifice;" that is, "Go back to your pupils," Knox having obtained a position of tutor to the sons of two families who had embraced reform principles.

Wishart was soon after taken to St. Andrews and burned, at which the people who had witnessed his martyrdom and sympathized with his views were so incensed that a company of men combined together and assassinated the archbishop, May 29, 1546, took possession of the castle, and made St. Andrews the stronghold of the reformers. The leaders among the Protestants did not approve of the assassination of Cardinal Beaton, and certainly did not advise it; yet there was little regret that it was done. Hence lampoons like the following were quite popular:

> "As for the cardinal, we grant,
> He was a man we weel might want,
> And we'll forget him sone;
> And yet I think, the sooth to say,
> Although the lown is weell away,
> The deed was foully done."

About a year after the death of Beaton, Knox, who was desirous of visiting Germany, was persuaded by the parents of his pupils to take refuge instead in the Castle of St. Andrews. While there he was elected pastor of the Protestants in St. Andrews, and was very successful; so that a large number of the garrison in the castle and many of the inhabitants of the town renounced Popery and professed the Protestant faith. But his work was soon ended, for, at the request of the regent of the kingdom, Mary of Guise, whose forces were attempting the capture of the castle in revenge for the murder of Beaton, a French fleet appeared before the town in June, 1547, and it was found necessary to capitulate.

Knox, with others, was taken to France, and condemned as a slave to the galleys. His captivity, which lasted for about eighteen months, was a hard one, and all the more so because he still maintained his Protestant principles; but he was in an especial manner upheld by the consolations of God's Spirit, and had an assured confidence that he would preach again at St. Andrews. When the galley on which he was employed visited the coast of Scotland in the summer of 1548, and he was asked by a fellow-prisoner, pointing to the spires of St. Andrews, if he thought he would ever visit the city again, he replied, "I am fully persuaded, how weak soever I now appear, that I shall not depart this life till that my tongue shall glorify His holy name in the same place." By-and-by he realized the hope with which he was inspired. In February, 1549, he was released, probably at the intercession of the English government, and immediately repaired to England.

Henry VIII. had been dead two years, and the boy, Edward VI., his successor, was favorable to the Reformation. Knox was known to the king's council of regency by reputation, and was well received by them, and soon appointed as preacher at Berwick. During the five years of his residence in England he held positions of large influence. At Berwick his fearless preaching against the idolatry of the Romish mass brought him into disfavor with Bishop Tunstall, who summoned him to give an account of his doctrines, but on hearing his vindication dismissed him without venturing to censure him. In the beginning of 1551, Knox was transferred to Newcastle; and at the end of the year he was made one of the six royal chaplains, and occasionally preached before the king. As royal chaplain he signed his name to the articles of religion drawn up by Cranmer as the standard of doctrine of the English Church. The bishopric of Rochester and the living of All Hallows, in London, were afterwards offered to Knox, but he declined them both, and had to answer before the privy council for so doing.

He rejected the bishopric because he believed "the episcopal office was destitute of divine authority, and inconsistent with the canons of the church herself." At St. Andrews he had taught, in opposition to popery, "that no mortal man could be the head of the church; that there were no true bishops but such as preached personally, without a substitute; that in religion men were bound to regulate themselves by divine laws; and that the sacraments ought to be administered exactly according to the institution and example of Christ;" and without repudiating some of these principles he felt that he could not become a bishop in the English Church, over which Henry VIII. had asserted a supremacy for the monarch of England much like that which the pope claimed over all Christendom.

Edward VI. died in July, 1553, and was succeeded by Mary. Protestant worship was prohibited, persecution was commenced, and Knox, at the urgent request of his friends, escaped to the Continent, landing at Dieppe in January, 1554. A short time previous to this he had either married or solemnly betrothed himself to Miss Marjory Bowes, of Berwick, but he had to leave England without even the opportunity of bidding her farewell. God led him finally to Geneva, where he was greatly gladdened by his intercourse with Calvin. From this place he went to Frankfort, and for a short time acted as pastor of the congregation of English refugees. After resigning his charge there, in March, 1555, on account of dissensions in the congregation in regard to usages of worship, he visited Scotland, and passed through a large part of it, secretly preaching in the houses of the faithful, and exhorting them to continue in the faith. In the summer of 1556, he went, with his wife and her mother, to Geneva, to become the pastor of the English congregation there, which included many who had taken his part in the disagreements at Frankfort.

At Geneva he remained two years, which were probably the quietest and fullest of enjoyment of all the years of his life. During this period, irritated by the fierce bigotry and unwearying cruelty of Bloody Mary, he wrote his treatise, "The First Blast of the Trumpet against the Monstrous Regiment of Women," in which he attempted to show that women had no right to the government of nations, etc. This pamphlet excited the enmity of Mary of England, and her successor Elizabeth, and also of Mary of Guise, queen-regent of Scotland, and her daughter Mary, the future queen. It would have been better if it had never been written.

Finally, at the request of the Protestant nobles, Knox returned to Scotland, arriving at Leith May 2, 1559. At the time of his arrival a provincial council was sitting in the monastery of the Greyfriars, in Edinburgh, concocting schemes to forward the interests of popery. When informed that John Knox had arrived, and that he had slept the preceding night in Edinburgh, the assembly was panic-stricken. A messenger was at once despatched to the regent, and Knox was proclaimed an outlaw and rebel.

A very short time after this Knox preached a sermon at Perth against the idolatry of the host and image-worship, and at its close, in consequence of an altercation between a priest and a boy, a spirit of violence was aroused, and the mob destroyed the images in the church, and tore down the monasteries. From Perth, Knox journeyed, preaching in the various towns on his way to St. Andrews, where, in accordance with his confident expectation while à galley-slave, he preached again "in that place where God first opened his mouth." Against the advice of friends and the threats of the archbishop, he determined to preach in the cathedral; and so powerful were the sermons that he delivered there, for four successive days, that the magistrates and citizens of St. Andrews established the reformed worship, destroyed the images and pictures in the churches, and laid the monasteries in ruins. Many other places followed the example of the cities already reformed.

The lords, or lay leaders, of the congregation, as the Scottish Protestants, united by a solemn covenant in defence of their faith, were now called, were successful against the troops of the regent. In the end of June they took possession of Edinburgh, and Knox was elected pastor of St. Giles' Church. He was soon, however, compelled to leave the city in consequence of its being surrendered to the regent's troops, and he undertook a preaching tour through the country, and accomplished much for the cause in which he embarked. A reward was publicly offered to any one who would apprehend or kill him; but God kept him in safety, and in October of this same year he took a leading part in a convention of nobles, barons, and representatives of the kingdom, where they, as far as they could, suspended the queen-regent from her position until the meeting of a free parliament. Knox held, and was not afraid to avow it, that rulers are invested with authority for the public good; that obedience is not due to them in anything contrary to the divine law; that the law of the land is superior to a prince, and that no class of men have a right to rule over the people without their consent.

The lords of the congregation obtained aid from England, now governed by Elizabeth, against the queen-regent and her Scotch Catholics and French allies; Leith was captured after a long siege, during which the queen-regent died; and the treaty of Edinburgh was signed, July 7, 1560, by which both the French and English troops evacuated Scotland, and its government was committed to a council of its lords. John Knox returned to his charge in Edinburgh; and in August the Scottish parliament there assembled abolished Popery, and established the Protestant religion, adopting a confession of faith drawn up chiefly by Knox. The privy council soon after commissioned Knox and three other ministers to draw up a plan of ecclesiastical government. The "Book of Policy" then prepared was approved by the first general assembly of the Church of Scotland, which met December 20, 1560, and is still known as the "First Book of Discipline."

The following year, 1561, Mary Stuart, lately widowed, was invited to assume the reins of government herself. The young queen arrived in Scotland from France full of prejudice against the Protestant religion, and prepared, by direct or indirect means, to restore Popery as the religion of the realm. One of her first steps was to summon the leading Scottish reformer to an interview in the palace of Holyrood. Knox boldly confronted her on this and other occasions, and though possibly not always as politic as prudence might have demanded, he was certainly honest and brave, and his efforts were crowned with wonderful success. Few men in any age could have mustered the courage to declare to their sovereign, in her own palace, as Knox did,

"If princes exceed their bounds, madam, no

doubt they may be resisted, even by power. For no greater honor or greater obedience is to be given to kings and princes than God has commanded to be given to father and mother. But the father may be struck with a frenzy, in which he would slay his children. Now, madam, if the children arise, join together, apprehend the father, take the sword from him, bind his hands, and keep him a prisoner till the frenzy be over, think you, madam, that the children do any wrong?"

"Well, then, I perceive that my subjects shall obey you, and not me, and will do what they please, and not what I command."

"God forbid," said the reformer, "that ever I take upon me to command any to obey me, or to set subjects at liberty to do whatever pleases them; but *my travail is, that both princes and subjects may obey God.*"

The contest between Popery, headed by Mary, and Protestantism, headed by Knox, went on, and Mary, despairing of moving the reformer by either flattery or tears, caused his indictment for treason, and herself appeared as prosecutrix of the charge at his trial before the privy council, in December, 1562. The trial resulted in Knox's discharge, and his commendation, by the majority of the noblemen present, for his judicious defence.

In March, 1564, Knox, having lost his first wife three years before, married Margaret Stewart, daughter of Lord Ochiltree, the ceremony being performed in a room which is still shown in Ochiltree House.

About a month after Queen Mary's marriage to Lord Darnley in the summer of 1565, a sermon preached by Knox at St. Giles' offended the young king, who was present, and occasioned the second summons of Knox before the privy council. The reformer, in his defence, declared that he had but followed his text, Isa. 26 : 13–21; but he was forbidden to preach again while the queen and her husband remained in Edinburgh. During the two years which intervened between this time and Mary's disgrace, Knox was engaged in the preparation of a *Historie of the Reformatioun*, in other literary labors, and in church visitations in the south of Scotland.

In July, 1567, he preached the sermon at the coronation, at Stirling, of the infant king, James VI., whose mother's nobles, as well Catholic as Protestant, shocked by her marriage with her husband's murderer Bothwell, had risen against their queen, imprisoned her in Lochleven Castle, and appointed her son her successor, and her half-brother, the Earl of Murray, regent of the kingdom.

The assassination of Murray in January, 1569, was a sore grief to the reformer, who preached the regent's funeral sermon on his interment in St. Giles'. Knox's health was already shaken by his many conflicts and trials, and a stroke of apoplexy further weakened him in October, 1570. He, however, recovered sufficiently to be able to preach again with his wonted faithfulness and vigor.

In the spring of 1571 religious and political strife prevailed with such violence in Edinburgh, and Knox had so excited the enmity of an influential party by the freedom of his utterances, that his friends urged his retirement to St. Andrews, where he accordingly spent fifteen months. After his return in weakness to Edinburgh in August, 1572, he was helped into the pulpit one day in the following September, and with all the energy that he could summon denounced the French king, Charles IX., for the terrible massacre of the Huguenots begun on St. Bartholomew's day, tidings of which event had just reached Scotland.

After appearing but once more in public, at the induction of his successor at St. Giles', the reformer's little remaining strength rapidly gave way, and he died on Monday the 24th of November, 1572. On the Wednesday following, the eulogy which we have already quoted was pronounced over his grave.

We close our sketch with the following extract from the volume of Dr. McCrie, to which we are partly indebted for the facts above related:

"He died in the sixty-seventh year of his age, not so much oppressed with years, as worn out and exhausted by his extraordinary labors of body and anxieties of mind. Few men were ever exposed to more dangers, or underwent greater hardships. From the time when he embraced the reformed religion till he breathed his last, seldom did he enjoy a respite from trouble; and he emerged from one scene of difficulty and danger only to be involved in another still more distressing. . . . . Yet he escaped all these perils, and finished his course in peace and in honor. No wonder that he was weary of the world, and anxious to depart; and with great propriety might it be said, at his decease, that 'he rested from his labors.'"

THOMAS CRANMER.

On the twenty-first of March, 1556, in the third year of the reign of Bloody Mary of England, a sad procession passed from the Bocardo prison to St. Mary's Church, Oxford. The first in the procession was the lord mayor, followed by the aldermen of the city, and after them two friars, mumbling psalms, and between them an old man, nearly seventy years of age, dressed in "a bare and ragged gown, and ill-favoredly clothed, with an old square cap." And yet this same man had been the primate of England, and the king's privy councillor—as compared with many of his compeers, a faithful minister of the gospel of the Lord Jesus Christ, and a reformer in the church. In his old age he had fallen into the hands of papal persecutors, and he need expect no mercy. Yet in fairness it must be stated that he, in common not only with the Church of Rome, but also with many truly pious Protestants of that intolerant age, held that death was the right punishment for misbelief; he had theoretically and practically favored the capital punishment of heretics: and in the judgment of those who tried him, *he* was a heretic. His career was a chequered one; and though he was not without grave faults, his connection with the Reformation renders his name worthy of remembrance.

Thomas Cranmer, the old man of whom we have spoken, was born in July, 1489, at Aslacton, Nottinghamshire, England; and, at the age of fourteen, was admitted a member of Jesus College, Cambridge. He was noted for patient study rather than brilliancy, and during his residence here he accumulated stores of information which proved of great value to him in after years. In 1528 he was at Waltham, as tutor of the sons of Mr. Cressy, at whose house he met Gardiner and Fox, two officers of the royal household of Henry VIII. In conversation with them he made some suggestions respecting the king's desired divorce from his wife, Catherine of Aragon, the widow of his brother Arthur. A dispensation had been obtained from the pope enabling Henry to marry Catherine, marriage with a brother's widow being assumed to be contrary to the law of God; but now that the king had fallen in love with Anne Boleyn, he claimed that he could not conscientiously live longer with Catherine as his wife. Pope Clement VII., however, refused to sanction a divorce; and Cranmer suggested submitting the question of the propriety of the marriage with Catherine to learned divines.

This suggestion being reported to the king, Cranmer was sent for, and empowered to procure the opinion of the universities and scholars of England and the Continent. This he accordingly did, making an extended tour for the purpose; and although he encountered much opposition, he succeeded in obtaining a sufficient showing in the king's favor to embolden Henry to take the matter into his own hands, assert his independence of the pope, and institute measures for the consummation of the divorce in England, on the ground that the former dispensation was unlawful. Thus God overruled the wicked passion of the king to further the Reformation.

King Henry, being pleased with Cranmer's diligence and ability in advocating the divorce, promoted him to the See of Canterbury. Thus he became metropolitan of England, and took the requisite oath of obedience to the pope, March 30, 1533, protesting, however, that "he did not intend, by this oath, to restrain himself from anything that he was bound to, either by his duty to God, or the king, or the country." The following May he declared the king's marriage void, and officiated a week later, June 1, at the coronation of the new queen, Anne Boleyn.

More edifying than Cranmer's connection with this and subsequent royal divorces, was the part which he took in causing the circulation of the Scriptures among the people. In December, 1534, he secured a resolution of the convocation, or assembly of the bishops and inferior clergy of England, in favor of a translation of the Bible. In 1537 he gained Henry's sanction for the publication of a version compiled by John Rogers from the translations of Tyndale and Coverdale; a revised edition of this work was published in 1540, and known as the "Cranmer Bible," because it contained an introduction by the primate. In 1534 Cranmer also delivered an address in the House of Lords respecting general councils, in which he said "he much doubted in himself respecting general councils, and thought that only the Word of God was the rule of faith which ought to take place in all controversies of religion. The Scriptures were called canonical, as being the only rule of the faith of Christians; and these, by the appointments of ancient councils, alone were to be read in the churches. The holy fathers, Ambrose, Jerome, and Augustine, in many things differed from one another; but they always appealed to the Scriptures as the common and certain standard."

Such conduct could not escape the notice of

the pope. Accordingly, in 1535, Pope Paul III. fulminated a terrific bull against Henry VIII., releasing the English from their oaths of fidelity, ordering the nobles to take up arms against the king, requiring the ecclesiastics to leave the kingdom, and prohibiting other nations from having any intercourse with England, under the severest penalties. The bull was treated with contempt, and the sacredness of such rescripts was no longer revered. Thus the people were being prepared for the Reformation.

The following year, largely through Cranmer's influence, "The Primer"—a collection of some thirty distinct tracts—was published, in which many of the leading doctrines of popery were attacked. But the publication of the several editions of the Bible did more than anything else to propagate the influence of the gospel in England, and Cranmer did much to facilitate their circulation. When he heard that his request for the royal authorization of the edition of 1537 had been granted, he wrote "that it afforded him more joy than the gift of a thousand pounds." It was through his influence that an order was given for the placing of an English Bible in every church, in a spot where it might be conveniently read by the people, many of whom resorted to the churches for the purpose.

The strict Romish party continued to oppose Cranmer and to labor for the full restoration to power of their agents; and they succeeded in 1539, through the influence of the Duke of Norfolk, in securing an enactment known as the "Six Articles," by which six of the principal errors of popery were again established, and agreement to them was required on pain of death. These articles sanctioned, first, the doctrine of transubstantiation; second, the Romish communion in one kind; third, priests were forbidden to marry; fourth, monastic vows were declared binding; fifth, private masses were allowed; sixth, confession was enjoined.

Cranmer was opposed to the measure, but as it was favored by King Henry, it became a law; and in less than fourteen days the prisons were full of witnesses for the truth, most of whom, however, through the exertions of the prime minister Cromwell, were released not long afterwards.

The year 1543 witnessed the publication of Cranmer's translation of the Litany into English, which formed the germ of the English prayer-book, a work completed, in substantially the same form in which it now exists, by Cranmer and a commission under him, in the reign of Edward VI.

Notwithstanding Cranmer's occasional opposition to the king, he had so won the regard of the monarch that Henry stood by him until his own death in July, 1547. Edward VI. succeeded his father, and during his reign the Reformation made great progress. Cranmer was encouraged by the young prince and by his uncle the lord-protector, Duke of Somerset, in every effort for the establishment of Protestantism; and, as a result, "the worship of images was prohibited; the saints and the virgin were no longer allowed to usurp any of that honor which is due to God alone; transubstantiation and the sacrifice of the mass were no longer substituted for the true doctrine and regular administration of the Lord's supper; the free use of the Scriptures in the vulgar tongue was permitted to persons of every rank and condition; human traditions were not referred to as equal or superior in authority to the Word of God; public prayers were no longer offered in an unknown tongue; the clergy were not prohibited from marriage," etc.

But Edward's reign lasted only some six years, and the great work could not be completed. Unfortunately an effort was made, in the interests of Protestantism, to place upon the throne Lady Jane Grey, a granddaughter of the younger sister of Henry VIII., instead of the legal heir, Mary, the daughter of Catherine of Aragon; and the result was the full identification of Mary with Popery after she obtained the crown. The progress of the Reformation was thereupon greatly hindered, and hundreds of its most godly defenders were made martyrs.

In March, 1554, Cranmer, who had incurred the heavy displeasure of Mary by his course in regard to her mother and herself, and by his recent support of Lady Jane Grey, was sent to prison at Oxford; there he was granted the mockery of a trial for heresy, was excommunicated, degraded from his archbishopric, and condemned to death. After his condemnation every artifice was resorted to by the Romish priesthood to induce him to recant; and dreading the fiery death that threatened him, he yielded, and signed no less than six recantations, each more abject than the preceding one.

On the 21st of March, 1556, the sad procession which we have already described took its way to St. Mary's Church, where Dr. Cole, after preaching a sermon on the mercy and justice of God, introduced Cranmer, that he might repeat his retraction before the assembled congregation. The old man kneeled in prayer, and then exhorted the people, concluding with the following words:

"Now I come to the great thing that so much troubleth my conscience, more than anything which I ever did or said in my whole life; and that is the setting abroad of writings contrary to the truth, and which now here I renounce and refuse as things written with my hand contrary to the truth which I thought in my heart, and which were written for fear of death, to save my life if it might be; and that is all such bills and papers which I have written or signed with my hand since my degradation, wherein I have written many things untrue. And forasmuch as my hand offended, writing contrary to my heart, my hand shall first be punished therefor; for when I come to the fire, it shall be burned first. And as for the pope, I refuse him as Christ's enemy, and Antichrist, with all his false doctrine."

This speech, so contrary to what was expected, filled the priests with rage, and Cole cried out, "Stop the heretic's mouth, and take him away!"

Soon he was dragged to the stake, and bound with a chain; and when the fire was kindled, he thrust his right hand into the flame, as he had promised, and with eyes lifted up to heaven, exclaimed, "Oh, this unworthy right hand!"

For twenty-seven years previous to his death he had done much for the cause of Christ and

Protestantism, and had in many respects well discharged the duties of the high positions which he occupied. It is easy to condemn many of his actions; but whether, with his light and surroundings, each one of us would have done better, is another question. "Let him that thinketh he standeth take heed lest he fall."

It has been truly said that "the key to his character is well given in what Hooper said of him in a letter to Bullinger, that he was '*too fearful about what might happen to him.*'" He had too great love of worldly ease and honor; too little trust in and devotion to God.

Of the effect of his death, Green says, in his "Short History of the English People," p. 374:

".... Among a crowd of far more heroic sufferers, the Protestants fixed, in spite of his recantations, on the martyrdom of Cranmer as the deathblow to Catholicism in England. For one man who felt within him the joy of Rowland Taylor at the prospect of the stake, there were thousands who felt the shuddering dread of Cranmer..... The sad pathos of the primate's humiliation and repentance struck chords of sympathy and pity in the hearts of all. It is from that moment that we may trace the bitter remembrance of the blood shed in the cause of Rome."

JOHN BUNYAN.

ALMOST at any time between the years 1660 and 1672 might be seen in a "damp den" in Bedford jail, England, a thoughtful prisoner, busy either tagging corset-laces, that he might aid in the support of his family, or perhaps with his pen writing down sentences of a work which should afterwards be published in almost every land and read in nearly every tongue. It was a strange place to produce such a work, and, as men judge, a strange man who had undertaken it. Nevertheless it was done, and the name of John Bunyan is now known as one of the world's great and good men.

Bunyan was born in the village of Elstow, near Bedford, in 1628. His life ran through that stormy period in English history which included the execution of Charles I., the Protectorate of one of England's greatest men, Oliver Cromwell, and ended with the Revolution of 1688. Bunyan's education was very meagre. It extended little, if at all, beyond reading and writing. He was evidently a bold, reckless boy; but his mind must early have been impressed with many of the truths of religion, for his conscience was even in

his wickedest days by no means seared, and it held him back from many a sin. He enlisted when about seventeen in the Parliamentary ranks, and no doubt was a brave soldier. At one time, while in the service, he was with others selected for some dangerous work at the siege of Leicester, but for some reason another soldier begged to be allowed to go in his place. The request was granted, the substitute was killed, and Bunyan, when he afterwards came to accept the doctrine that "God's kingdom ruleth over all"—"that a sparrow cannot fall to the ground without his knowledge"—was devoutly thankful that the Lord had in this way, and in other ways and times, saved him from death.

He married while quite young, and his wife seems to have exerted a good influence over him, and succeeded in taking him to the parish church with her, at least for the forenoon services. In the afternoon he preferred a game of ball on the village green to the services of the sanctuary; but on one particular Sabbath the parish minister preached on the profanation of the Sabbath, a sermon which greatly impressed Bunyan. The impression wore off before he had quite finished his dinner, and he went to his usual sport on the green; but in the midst of the game, while he was striking the cat with his bat, it seemed to him that a voice suddenly broke into his soul, saying, "Wilt thou leave thy sins and go to heaven, or have thy sins and go to hell?" The sequence of this appeal of God's Spirit was at the time a fit of despair. Bunyan concluded that he would be lost, and so gave himself up to wickedness, and especially to the use of profane language, in which he indulged so freely that he was one day reproved by a woman of bad character, who told him that "his words made her tremble." Conviction followed her reproof, and from that time he abandoned this ungodly practice. Some conversation on religion and the Bible led him to take an interest in reading the Scriptures, and to be still more particular in regard to his behavior. His neighbors noticed the change in his conduct, and began to speak of it; and afterwards he wrote concerning it, "Though as yet I was nothing but a poor painted hypocrite, yet I loved to be talked of as one that was truly godly."

Fear took possession of his soul, so that he did not dare ring the church bell, an amusement he was very fond of, lest the steeple should fall, and he be brought face to face with that God whom he had so often offended. But he says, in his "Grace Abounding," that in the good providence of God he went to Bedford in the pursuit of his calling as "a travelling tinker," and while passing slowly down one of the streets of that town he heard a few women talking about "the things of God," and soon discovered that they had a knowledge and joy which he did not possess. From their conversation he was led to study the Scriptures with new earnestness, and to pray that God would enlighten his darkness. He had, however, many conflicts with Satan before he was enabled to rejoice in the light of the knowledge that Christ was his Saviour. The tempter suggested that he was not one of the elect, and that therefore it was impossible that he could be saved. But the words in Luke 14 : 22 saved him from despair. "'Yet there is room' were sweet words to me," he said. "I thought that by them I saw that there was place enough in heaven for me."

But he experienced after this many troubles and trials, many lights and shadows; sometimes he rejoiced in God, and at other times mourned as one for ever shut out from his favor. Finally, Satan so followed him with the temptation to "sell Christ," as Judas had done, that he yielded so far as to say, "Let him go if he will." Then darkness surrounded him; he thought he had committed the unpardonable sin. But the Spirit of God applied to his heart the declaration, "The blood of Jesus Christ his Son cleanseth us from *all sin*," and again peace and joy filled his heart.

In 1653 he was baptized by Rev. Mr. Gifford, the Baptist minister at Bedford, the "Evangelist" of the "Pilgrim," to whom, as well as to Luther's Commentary on the Galatians, Bunyan was greatly indebted for instruction. Two or three years later, at the urgent request of members of the Baptist congregation, he began to exhort, at first with great diffidence, and privately in small assemblies, but afterwards with more courage and publicity, as he became convinced that God was helping him and blessing his ministrations. He was, ere long, solemnly commissioned to preach, and, while still working at his trade, itinerated as an evangelist in the villages about Bedford, multitudes flocking to hear him. But after preaching about five years, he was arrested in November, 1660, for holding unlawful meetings, and not conforming to the usages of the Episcopal Church, which, with the restoration of Charles II., had again become the established church of England. To use his own words, Bunyan was taken "home to prison" because he would not cease telling lost men the way of salvation through a crucified Redeemer.

Previous to this his first wife had died, leaving him four children, one of whom was blind. He was now married again to an excellent woman, who made strenuous efforts to secure his release from prison, but in vain. One of his greatest sorrows, previous to his imprisonment (for he had expected arrest for some time), was the anticipation of leaving his wife and poor children to the mercy of a cold world. The realization of this dread was the source of keen suffering to him while imprisoned. "I have," he wrote, "found myself a man encompassed with infirmities; the parting with my wife and poor children hath often been to me in this place as pulling the flesh from the bones; and that not only because I am somewhat too fond of these great mercies, but also because I would have often brought to my mind the many hardships, miseries, and wants that my poor family would be like to meet with should I be taken from them, especially my poor blind child, who lay nearer to my heart than all besides. Oh, the thought of the hardships my poor blind one might undergo would break my heart to pieces." But in such a time he remembered the promise, "Leave thy fatherless children; I will preserve them alive; and let thy widows trust in me." And so, in spite of all his fears, he witnessed a good confession for his Master, and patiently bore the long years of his imprisonment in Bedford jail. Here his blind daughter was often permitted to visit him, and to carry home to her mother the tagged stay-laces at which he had been working.

An anonymous writer describes the scene in simple verse so tenderly that we cannot help quoting it:

"Now go, my child; the parting hour
  Is all too swiftly come;
The quiet evening closes in,
  And thou must hasten home.

"Ay, now the darkness and the light
  Are not alike to thee;
The darkness steals thee from thy rest
  Against thy father's knee.

"And when the first star twinkles through
  My prison bars from high,
We kneel upon the cold stone floor,
  My little child and I.

"And with thy dear hands clasped in mine,
  So tiny and so fair,
With prison walls around us both,
  I hear thy evening prayer.

"Now it is ended, and the star
  Warns me to say farewell;
I may not keep thee longer here
  Within my lonely cell.

"And thou must carry home the work
  Thy father's hand hath wrought;
Each thread I wove grew beautiful
  With some home-pictured thought.

"Child, pass thy little hand across
  Thy mother's brow to-night,
And tell me if the lines grow deep,
  Or tears bedim her sight;

"And notice if her voice be sad,
    And if her steps be slow;
Although their soft, low echoings
    Are cheery here below.

"Child, thou hast made my prison-house
    So bright for many an hour!
Now haste thee to thy mother's arms,
    My little prison flower!

"For she is watching for thee, dear;
    I see her standing there;
The ruddy glow of firelight
    Gleams on my empty chair.

"And I shall meet you all to-night
    Before God's mercy-seat;
When, kneeling midst her little ones,
    She prays at Jesus' feet.

"I would that I could join you all,
    As sinks the setting sun,
To pray as we were wont to do;
    But God's good will be done!

"Oh, when the light of heaven shall be
    My Mary, on thy sight;
And, hand in hand, we wander on
    In rapturous delight,

"How sweet and fond the memory
    Of these long hours will be,
Which I have spent in prison-cell,
    My darling child, with thee!

"Thou wilt remember all the gloom
    Of this long, darksome night,
Only to make thy Saviour's home
    More gloriously bright.

"For each dark hour, my Mary, here,
  That God to thee hath given,
Are treasured up bright ages there,
  Thy heritage in heaven.

"But, hark! I hear the gaoler's step;
  Yon star is growing bright;
God bless thee, and thou shalt be blessed!
  Good night, my child, good night!"

But the tagging of corset-laces was not all his work. He formed a little congregation from the inmates of his prison, studied his Bible and Fox's "Book of Martyrs," and wrote evangelistic and controversial tracts. It was during these twelve years of imprisonment that he produced the first part of his immortal book, "The Pilgrim's Progress," a work which led Lord Macaulay to class him side by side with Milton, as the second of the two great imaginative writers of the seventeenth century. During the last four years of his detention he enjoyed a great deal of liberty, being allowed to attend the Baptist meetings, and even, in the last year, to officiate as pastor of the congregation, indulgences due to the respect and pity which he had won by his character and sufferings.

In 1672 the Declaration of Indulgence, suspending all penal laws against Nonconformists—a measure by which Charles II. hoped to advance towards his secret aim of reëstablishing Catholicism in England—opened many prison doors, and allowed Bunyan and others to go free. And now, for some sixteen years, apparently without let or hindrance other than is usual in the work of the ministry, he engaged with zeal in this, to him, blessed work. On his yearly visit to London, thousands crowded to hear him tell of the wisdom and necessity of leaving the city of destruction and travelling to the celestial city. His pen was also busy, and his "Grace Abounding," "Jerusalem Sinner Saved," and other works, still point sinners to the cross, that they may lose their burden, and with joyful heart pass on their journey heavenward; while his "Heavenly Footman" and his "Holy War" show what God-given wisdom, earnestness, and strength are needful for the winning of the Christian race and warfare.

Finally, after accomplishing a labor of love—the reconciliation of a father and son—Bunyan was seized with a fever at a friend's house in London, and after an illness of ten days died on the 31st of August, 1688, less than three months before William of Orange landed in England. He was buried in Bunhill Fields, London, where his dust awaits the coming of the Divine Redeemer to raise it in honor and glory.

BERNARD PALISSY.

Towards the close of the sixteenth century King Henry III. visited, in a prison of his capital, a noble old man, of whose life and discoveries France to-day is proud, and urged him to abjure his religion, that his life might be saved. He said, "I am compelled to deliver you into the hands of your enemies, and to-morrow you will be burned unless you are converted." But Palissy, then nearly eighty years of age, nobly replied, "I am ready to give up the remainder of my life for the honor of God; you have told me several times that you pity me, and now, in my turn, I pity you who have used the words, 'I am compelled.' It is not spoken like a king, sire; and they are words which neither you, nor the Guises, nor the people, can ever make me utter. *I can die.*" Noble words from the lips of the old Huguenot, Palissy the potter.

What inspired him with such heroism? How did he come to be in prison and to be visited by a king? We shall see.

Bernard Palissy was born at La Chapelle Biron, near Agen, in 1510, just ten years before Luther burned the pope's bull at Wittenberg, and some sixty-two years before the massacre of St. Bartholomew; accordingly, by the time Palissy became of age and had finished his apprenticeship to the business of glazing, the country was ablaze with discussions on questions of religion. In 1539, when he was twenty-nine years of age, it was made a crime, punishable with death, in France, to read the Bible. But even such an edict had no controlling effect upon a mind so independent and inquiring as was his.

At the completion of his apprenticeship he undertook a journey through the country adjacent to the Pyrenees, and through the provinces of the lower Rhine, sustaining himself by engaging in his trade and painting on glass. In his journeying he met many warm adherents of the reformed faith, learned to read the newly-printed Bible, and, better still, to love its precepts; and, on his return to Saintes, he commenced the work of an exhorter, in accordance with the good example, counsel, and doctrine of the worthy Philibert Hamelin, a noble laborer, who was afterwards condemned as a heretic, and put to death at Bordeaux. Following his example, Palissy associated with himself some six others, and alternately they read and expounded the Scriptures to as many as they could assemble from Sabbath to Sabbath, in their private meetings, for they dared not meet openly. In these meetings Palissy was much comforted and encouraged, and prepared for his patient labor during the week.

At that period he specially needed encouragement. Some years previously, having seen a beautiful enamelled cup of Italian manufacture, he was seized with a desire to obtain the secret of the art. At great cost of time and labor, amid the jeers and scoffs of his neighbors, and, worse still, the reproaches of his wife and children, he patiently experimented, until, after sixteen years of persevering toil, the secret was obtained. These years were years of poverty, sorrow, and distress for himself and his family, and he needed the comforts of religion to sustain him until his triumph came, and earthly glory and wealth were showered upon him. After his success he removed to Paris, and was honored with the friendship of nobles and princes. But while he was struggling for his secret, he sought the consolations which he needed in communion with his Saviour; nor was he content to enjoy these blessings for himself: he sought to bring others to a knowledge of the same soul-sustaining and saving truths, and so he formed the first Reformed church of Saintes. Few and despised were its members at the first, and rumor charged them with all kinds of wickedness; but their upright lives at length impressed their neighbors, and Catholics soon began to say to their priests, "See these ministers of the new religion; they make prayers, they lead a holy life; why cannot you do the like?" and the result was that more began to favor and practise the precepts of Protestantism. Palissy, years after, described the advance of the Reformed faith as follows:

"In those days might be seen, on Sundays, bands of work-people walking abroad in the meadows, the groves, and the fields, singing psalms and spiritual songs, or reading to and instructing one another. There might also be seen girls and maidens, seated in groups in the gardens and pleasant places, singing songs on sacred themes; or boys, accompanied by their teachers, the effects of whose instruction had already been so salutary that these young people not only exhibited a manly bearing, but a manful steadfastness of conduct. Indeed, these various influences, working one with another, had already effected so much good, that not only had the habits and modes of life of the people been reformed, but their very countenances themselves seemed to be changed and improved."

But the new religion, as it was called, was making similar progress in other portions of France, and the leaders of the Romish church took the alarm. Pope Pius IV., aided by Philip II. of Spain, urged the French authorities to interfere, to stay the progress of that gospel which was leading men to trust in the Lord Jesus Christ, and lead holy lives. The gospel faith was heresy, its adversaries declared; it would destroy both the church and the state.

Accordingly, in 1559, a royal edict was published by Henry II., declaring the crime of heresy punishable by death, and forbidding the judges to remit or mitigate the penalty. For a time Palissy concealed himself, in the hope that the storm of wrath would soon pass over; but he was too prominent a man, and too heartily devoted to the cause of the Reformation, to escape for any length of time. He was finally apprehended, and hurried by night to Bordeaux, to be tried for the crime of heresy, as his teacher Hamelin had been. No doubt he, too, would have been condemned and burned, if he had not been needed by the Catholic party. But the Duke of Montmorency was in urgent want of enamelled tiles for his castle-floor, and Palissy was the only man in France capable of producing them. The skill that God had given him, and that he had improved by faithful labor, was the cause of his deliverance. It was also the means of his advancement to the favor of the cunning and unprincipled Catherine de' Medici, wife of Henry II., and mother of the three succeeding kings of France, Francis II., Charles IX., and Henry III.

Palissy was appointed "maker of the king's rustic potteries," and a residence in the Tuileries was assigned to him. In the dreadful massacre of St. Bartholomew's day, in 1572, Catherine protected him from the fate which overwhelmed so many Protestants.

But neither royal favors nor royal frowns could shake Palissy's devotion to his religion, or lead him to dissemble. Christ and his Word had sustained him in the days of adversity, and he adhered to them in his prosperity.

Such was his faithfulness that he was, after a while, again apprehended, and thrown into the Bastile, where, as we have already said, he was visited by Henry III., to whom he boldly declared that, though he could not give up his religion, he "knew how to die." He was not, however, burned, but allowed to remain in his cell until, in 1589, death came to his release. Thus one of France's noblest martyrs witnessed for the truths of Christianity.

HENRY MARTYN.

In the year 1809, in Cawnpore, India, now celebrated as the place where so many English residents and missionaries were massacred at the beginning of the Sepoy rebellion of 1857, a noble missionary, one of more than ordinary gifts and graces, one who had obtained at the close of his college course the honor of senior wrangler at Cambridge, England, wrote a letter, of which the following is an extract: "What is there now that I should wish to live for? Oh, what a barren desert, what a howling wilderness does this world appear! But for the service of God in his church and the preparation of my own soul, I do not know that I should wish to live another day."

This missionary had just received intelligence from England of the death of a beloved sister, a sister who had been the means of leading him to Christ, and, as a consequence, one means of securing him for the mission work of India.

Henry Martyn was born in Truro, in the county of Cornwall, England, in February, 1781, over a hundred years ago. He entered the grammar-school of the town in his seventh year, and, notwithstanding his feeble constitution, "his proficiency in the classics exceeded that of most of his schoolfellows." His father had struggled hard to procure an education for himself, and he determined to aid his son in obtaining one. Accordingly, Henry was sent to St. John's College, Cambridge, in October, 1797. While there, the sister to whom we have already alluded exerted a happy influence over him, both by her letters and her conversation at home during his vacations. Referring afterwards to one of these conversations, he said,

"I do not remember a time in which the wickedness of my heart rose to a greater height than during my stay at home; the consummate selfishness and exquisite irritability of my mind were displayed in rage, malice, and envy, in pride and vainglory, and in contempt of all; in the harshest language to my sister, and even to my father, if he happened to differ from my mind and will."

But by-and-by that loving father was called home; and then what anguish filled the selfish heart of the son! The event was made, however, the means of leading him to consider the claims of the religion of Christ; and soon after he wrote to his sister that new light had dawned upon his mind. His words are, "I began to attend more diligently to the words of our Saviour in the New

Testament, and to devour them with delight, etc. I have only to express my acquiescence in most of your opinions, and to join with you in gratitude to God for his mercies to us. May he preserve you and me, and all of us, to the day of the Lord."

His course at Cambridge was now near its close, and he was preparing with much earnestness for the final contest; but he could now cast his cares on his unseen Friend, and doing so was all the better prepared for his examination. He experienced the truth of the declaration, "Thou wilt keep him in perfect peace whose mind is stayed on thee, because he trusteth in thee." He was successful in passing his examinations, and obtained the highest honor, that of "senior wrangler." But he soon after wrote, "I obtained my highest wishes, but was surprised to find that I had grasped a shadow." Most true it is that neither the world's wealth nor its honor can supply the cravings of an immortal soul.

He returned to Cambridge again to pursue studies with reference to a fellowship, which he succeeded in obtaining in 1802. During this period the Rev. Mr. Simeon became very much interested in him, and, aided by intercourse with him and other Christian friends, Martyn made great progress in the divine life, and soon could write to his sister, "Blessed be God, I have now experienced that Christ is the power of God and the wisdom of God. What a blessing is the gospel! No heart can conceive its excellency but that which has been renewed by divine grace." With these new experiences he became a faithful witness for Christ. He was never afraid or ashamed to rebuke flagrant sin; and in one case mentioned in the letter last quoted from, his remonstrance was, by the blessing of God, so effectual that the student rebuked afterwards became a bosom friend and a companion in the mission-work in India.

In the same year in which Martyn's fellowship was obtained, Mr. Simeon, to whom he was now greatly attached, made some remarks on the benefits that had resulted from the services of a single missionary; and the views which he presented induced Martyn to devote himself to the missionary cause. Accordingly, he applied to the society in London for an appointment "to any part of the world whither it might be convenient to send him."

In a journal, which he kept at this period, many interesting entries are found, showing his growth in Christian knowledge and grace. Of these the following is a specimen: "I read Hebrew, and the Greek of the Epistle to the Hebrews. This epistle is not only not uninteresting, as it formerly was, but it is now the sweetest portion of the Holy Scriptures I know: mostly, I suppose, because I can look up to Jesus as my High Priest, though I may very often doubt whether I am interested in him. Yet, oh, how free is his love to the chief of sinners! How many of my days are lost if their worth is to be measured by the standard of prevailing heavenly-mindedness! I want above all things a willingness to be despised. What but the humbling influence of the Spirit, showing me my vileness and desperate wickedness, can ever produce such an habitual temper!"

Mr. Martyn was ordained a deacon of the Church of England October 22, 1803, and began his ministerial work as curate to Mr. Simeon. He also took charge of the small parish of Lolworth, a few miles distant from Cambridge. His purpose was to labor in these fields until the Board at London should deem it proper to send him away as a missionary. In consequence of his superior scholarship, he was several times appointed to the honorable office of examiner in his college, and discharged it with much acceptance. Had he chosen to remain in England, honor and wealth were, humanly speaking, within his grasp; but he had already testified, when he obtained the senior wranglership, that such things did not satisfy the cravings of his soul.

At length Mr. Martyn received an appointment as chaplain to the East India Company, and began making preparations to leave his native land. He visited his old home in Cornwall, and preached. Crowds gathered to hear him, including his two sisters, the younger of whom we have already spoken of as a noble Christian woman; the other was as yet ignorant of Christ as her Saviour, but seemed to be greatly impressed with the preaching of her brother; and finally, before her death, she gave evidence that she loved and trusted the Saviour whom he so lovingly commended.

Mr. Martyn, having attained his twenty-fourth year, was ordained a presbyter in March, 1805, in St. James' Chapel, London. On the 3d of April he preached his farewell sermon "in the dear abode of his youth," where he had been so greatly loved and honored, and then took his departure for London, ready to embark on what was then considered a journey of danger, if not of death. Hence he wrote in his journal, June 11, "Shed tears to-night at the thought of my departure. I thought of the rolling seas which would soon be between me and all that is dear to me upon earth." He was going forth to preach to the heathen, not only "not knowing the things which should befall him," but with the settled determination never to return to England, but to die in the field of his labor, for Christ's sake.

On the 17th of July, 1805, the vessel in which he was to proceed to India sailed from Portsmouth, and, after many delays and stoppages by the way, he arrived at Madras April 22, 1806. Soon after he reached Calcutta, where he wrote, "My long and wearisome journey is concluded, and I have at last arrived in the country in which I am to spend my days in the work of the Lord. Scarcely can I believe myself to be so happy as to be actually in India; yet this hath God wrought." At Aldeen, near Calcutta, the residence of Rev. David Brown, Mr. Martyn was received with affectionate kindness. He at once began the study of the Hindostanee language, and at the same time was assiduous in preaching the gospel to his own countrymen.

On the 13th of September following he received his appointment to Dinapore. On his arrival there he began to establish native schools, to translate the Scriptures, and to endeavor to obtain such a knowledge of the language as would enable him to preach the gospel fluently in it. He found, as every missionary will, many unexpected obstacles in the way of prosecuting his work; and not the least among them was the godless character of resident Europeans, whom the natives regarded as Christians. But he labored on, occasionally encouraged by hopeful signs, and at other times crying out, "Who hath believed our report? and to whom is the arm of the Lord revealed?"

At length, in March, 1808, his translation of the New Testament into Hindostanee was completed, a work which still preaches the gospel, though Mr. Martyn was long ago transferred from the service of earth to that of heaven. Soon after this translation was finished he removed from Dinapore to Cawnpore, where he engaged in work similar to that already performed, and where he received the news of his sister's death, which occasioned the writing of the letter quoted from at the opening of this sketch. His older sister had died a year earlier.

At the close of the year 1809 he writes: "Ten years have elapsed since I was first called of God to the fellowship of the gospel, and ten times greater than ever ought to be my gratitude to the tender mercy of my God for all that he has done for me. The ways of wisdom appear more sweet and reasonable than ever, and the world more insipid and vexatious. The chief thing I have to mourn over is my want of power and fervor in secret prayer, especially when attempting to plead for the heathen."

At Cawnpore he prosecuted the work of translating the New Testament into Arabic, and also into Persian. It was found, however, that the Persian translation was not as good as was desirable; and this circumstance led Mr. Martyn to undertake a journey to Persia, to secure such a knowledge of the language as should enable him to prepare a version suitable for the people of that country. Accordingly, "on the 7th of January, 1811, after having preached a sermon on the anniversary of the Calcutta Bible Society," and after having addressed the inhabitants of Calcutta for the last time, from the text, "But one thing is needful," he departed for ever from the shores of India, where he had expected to end his days. But though he lived in that land for only a few years, he set in motion influences which will ever flow on to bless her inhabitants.

Mr. Martyn set out for Shiraz, Persia, January 7, and arrived at that celebrated seat of Persian literature June 9. A much shorter time would now suffice for the journey, but it must be remembered that we are speaking of over half a century ago. By the 24th of February of the following year (1812) Mr. Martyn had completed the Persian New Testament. He finished a version of the

Psalms a few weeks after. During this time he had also been much engaged in disputes with infidels and with the Mohammedans around him; and he had conducted his share of the discussions with such good-humor and acuteness that his opponents, in spite of their bigotry, confessed their love for him, and testified to the great ability with which he defended Christianity. It is believed that he was then permitted to sow seed which was afterwards to bring forth fruit to the glory of God.

But his health failed, and with the consciousness that his work was nearly done he turned his face homeward, intending to pass through Constantinople. He reached Tocat, in Asia Minor, and died, as was supposed, from the plague, which was then raging and depopulating the cities around. On the 16th of October, 1812, in the thirty-second year of his age, this faithful laborer breathed his last. His career was short, but he accomplished a great work, and made the work of other missionaries by so much the easier. God had endowed him with great talents, and he laid them all at the feet of the Master. It was said of him, "He always lived so that he could pray;" and thus he could and did bring down power from above to help him and others in the work of the Lord.

ADONIRAM JUDSON.

More than seventy years ago a young man, who had lately graduated with the highest honors at Brown University, left his father's house at Plymouth, Mass., to make a tour through some of the States on horseback. He was the dearly-beloved son of godly parents, who hoped, and, no doubt, frequently prayed, that the God in whom they trusted would be pleased to use their child as an instrument in building up the divine cause and kingdom in this world. They were, therefore, exceedingly troubled by the young man's open declaration, previous to leaving on his trip, that he did not believe the Bible which they reverenced so much—it was a "lot of old wives' fables." It was a sad parting, for these loving parents did not know that this journey was only a step in the preparation of their son to be one of the heroes of the church in the work of foreign missions. Those who are forgiven much love much, and this undutiful, proud, wayward son was soon to be brought a penitent to the feet of the Saviour; then, pardon having been obtained, he was, with loving and devoted heart, to tell

many perishing ones of the Saviour who had found him, and saved him by His grace.

By-and-by, in pursuing his journey, he reached a country tavern not far from Sheffield, N. Y., and obtained lodging for the night. The landlord apologized for placing him in a room next to one occupied by a young man supposed to be dying. He assured the landlord that it was a matter of no moment to him; but notwithstanding his bold assertions—his whistling to keep his courage up—he could not sleep; the sounds from the dying-bed fell upon his ear, and recalled the old teachings of his childhood. He thought of the preparation necessary for dying. He questioned, "What if there is a heaven and a hell? What if my mother's Bible is true? Suppose I were dying, how should I feel?" And then, to banish these unwelcome thoughts, he thought of his special friend at the university, E——, the leader of their infidel club; what would he think of such weakness as had just seized his mind? Ah, he did not then know what the coming morning revealed, that the dying youth, so hopeless and helpless, was just that very E——, and that his boasted reason and philosophy had done nothing for him in his dread encounter with the king of terrors.

Oppressed with the thought that his friend

was not only dead, but lost, the traveller determined, like the prodigal, to "arise and go to his father." The pride of philosophy was now gone; he wanted a mother's prayers and a father's counsel, and, above all, a Saviour's pardon. So he turned his horse's head to Plymouth again; and in the month of May, 1809, Adoniram Judson professed his faith in the Lord Jesus Christ as his Saviour, by uniting with the Third Congregational Church of Plymouth, of which his father was then pastor; and within less than a year afterwards he determined to go to the heathen to tell the story of divine grace.

Without a pang he turned away from all his ambitious plans, and determined to become a minister of the gospel of the grace of God. He continued his studies in Andover Theological Seminary, which he had entered soon after his return from New York; and there he met Nott and Newell, and after a while Gordon Hall and Mills. In different colleges God's Spirit had been moving the hearts of these young men, and inclining them to devote themselves to the noble work of carrying the gospel to the ends of the earth; and now, when they met together in the same seminary, Christian intercourse with one another kindled the zeal of each into a flame.

The work of foreign missions had as yet received little attention in America. Mr. Judson, therefore, wrote to England, to the venerable Dr. Bogue, to ascertain if he and his friends could be employed as missionaries by the London Missionary Society. But God's Spirit was stirring up an interest in the cause of foreign missions in the hearts of pastors and people here at home, as well as of students. Accordingly, Drs. Spring and Worcester, on their way to the General Congregational Association in session at Bradford, June 26, 1810, began to talk concerning the matter, and made the first suggestion towards forming "the American Board of Commissioners for Foreign Missions."

Messrs. Judson, Nott, Mills, and Newell presented to this same association a paper asking "advice, direction, and prayer" with reference to the work. The result of this appeal and of the suggestion before referred to was the noble institution which we have already named, which has done, and is still doing, so much to bring heathen nations under the sway of King Immanuel.

The money necessary to send out missionaries not being forthcoming at once, Mr. Judson, by advice of the prudential committee, sailed for England in 1811, to confer with the board of the London Missionary Society concerning the matter. At this period England and France were at war; the vessel in which Judson sailed was captured by a French privateer, and he was thrust with others into a dismal underground dungeon at Bayonne. Thus early was he inured to the terrible sufferings to which he would by-and-by be called in the work of his Master. He soon, however, reached his destination. His undertaking was successful to a certain degree, and became the means of stirring up the zeal of the friends of missions at home, so that at the next meeting of the American Board Messrs. Judson, Nott, Newell, and Hall were appointed missionaries to the Burman Empire, under the direction of the Prudential Committee, and on February 19, 1812, they embarked for India.

A few days previous to this, Mr. Judson married one of the noblest of American women, Ann Hasseltine, one who, by her heroic services, did almost as much as her husband to lay the foundation of mission work in Burmah. On the 6th of the same month a missionary meeting was held in Salem, Mass., for the service connected with the ordination and departure of the young missionaries. It was a great day for the cause; a new impulse was given by it to mission work throughout the entire land. Dr. Spring's declaration, then made, was soon accepted everywhere as the very truth: "No enterprise comparable to this has been embraced by the American church; all others retire before it, like the stars before the rising sun."

During the voyage to Calcutta, Mr. Judson examined the question of infant baptism, and adopted the theory of the Baptists, which made it necessary for him to resign his position as a missionary of the American Board, and thus also made it necessary to labor in a different field from that of his beloved brethren who accompanied him. The sacrifice involved in such a step cannot be fully understood by us at the present day. Denominational lines have become so much less conspicuous that we can scarcely understand the question which Mrs. Judson asked in a letter then written to a dear friend: "Can you, my dear Nancy, still love me, still desire to hear from me, when I tell you I have become a Baptist?"

Another source of trouble opened before these young missionaries in the opposition of the East India Company. Scarcely ten days had elapsed after their arrival when they were ordered by the government to return to America in the ship which had brought them out. It was strange that that English company should be so afraid of missionaries as to exert all its power to prevent them from landing on the shores of India. But for the missionary and his work, England would not to-day have so secure a foothold in India. Judson lived, however, to be protected and treated like a prince by some of England's chief officers, and no people now appreciate more fully than the English the value of missionary services, and their tendency to give stability to civil government. But at that early period of darkness the missionary had to suffer; and, accordingly, Judson was driven from the country. I wonder that some artist has not painted a picture of Messrs. Judson and Rice, together with Mrs. Judson, stealing at midnight through the streets of Calcutta, followed by coolies carrying their baggage, to reach a vessel in the dock about to sail for the Isle of France (Mauritius).

Finally, in July, 1813, Mr. and Mrs. Judson reached Rangoon, then in the Burman empire, now included in the British Presidency of Bengal. Here Mr. Judson, ably assisted by his wife, labored and prayed and suffered, learned the language, translated portions of the New Testament, and finally preached. At last, five years after he began his work, "the firstfruits of Christ's church in Burmah were gathered in the conversion of Moung Nau." But now the little one has become a thousand, and the small one almost a nation. His preparatory labor was not in vain. It was the sowing before the harvest of sheaves.

In 1821 Mrs. Judson was compelled, by the loss of health, to return to America, and in her absence Mr. Judson busied himself in translating additional portions of the New Testament. Some months after her departure he was summoned, together with Dr. Price, a missionary physician, who had some time before joined the mission, and whose fame as a surgeon had reached to Ava, to appear before the emperor. The missionary and the surgeon were received with much kindness, and the prospect of accomplishing great things in Ava for the cause of Christ appeared bright indeed.

Dr. Judson returned to Rangoon in the autumn of 1823, to meet Mrs. Judson on her return from America. On her arrival, with high expectations they left the mission under the care of fellow-laborers who had from time to time been sent out to aid them in their work, and went up the Irrawaddy to Ava.

Unfortunately, from our standpoint, but happily, no doubt, from the standpoint of the Lord Jesus Christ, who rules the world, war broke out between England and Burmah; and Dr. Price and Dr. Judson were both imprisoned as spies, and were held as prisoners in filthy dungeons some seventeen months, being frequently confined in fetters, and treated like dogs. They were finally ordered to be executed; but the death of the principal officer on the very morning appointed for their execution saved their lives.

Throughout this trying time Mrs. Judson displayed a heroism that has never been excelled, in striving to secure the liberty of her husband, and ministering to his wants; and had it not been for her exertions he would never have lived through the ordeal of his imprisonment. And yet, during those terrible days of sorrow and suffering, she was called to endure the pains of maternity, followed some time after by fever, which rendered her unable to nourish her little infant; but she succeeded in bribing the jailer to allow Dr. Judson to leave the prison for a short time each day to carry the poor child around the city, to beg a little nourishment from those mothers who had young children. No milk could be obtained otherwise, and the cries of the poor child through the night, writes the suffering mother, were heart-rending.

But by-and-by the end came, and Dr. Judson and his noble wife were received and treated, as we have already hinted, in princely style, by the English commander-in-chief, Sir Archibald Campbell, who also secured reparation for the property lost by them during the terrible months of persecution. The settlement of the war gave the English a large amount of territory, and a town at the mouth of the Salwen was selected as its capital, and named Amherst.

Encouraged and invited by the authorities, Dr. Judson removed to Amherst to found a new mission. Before the work was fully commenced, he was induced to go to the Burman court with the British envoy for the purpose of settling governmental business, and with the hope of securing toleration in the future for the Christian religion. During his absence on this important business, Mrs. Judson was summoned to a higher court, the home of her Heavenly Father; and just six months later, in May, 1827, the messenger returned for little Maria, the baby of whom we have spoken.

Desolate indeed did Amherst appear to 'Dr. Judson on his return; but he at once began his work of preaching, tract-writing, and translating; and in Prome, Rangoon, and Maulmain, he abounded in labors for the lost around him.

In 1828 his attention was turned to the Karens, the rude inhabitants of the interior jungles and mountains. They received the gospel gladly, and within twenty-five years after they heard it first, the converts among them were estimated at twenty thousand.

Dr. Judson soon became satisfied that but little progress could be made without the agency of the press; accordingly, he published tracts, portions of Scripture, etc., and finally, in January, 1834, he completed the translation of the whole Bible. Such is the excellence of this translation that it is claimed that it will be in the future "the Bible of Burmah."

In April, 1834, Dr. Judson married Mrs. Sarah H. Boardman, the widow of a missionary. This lady had been exceedingly active and useful in work among the Karens, instructing them in her school at Tavoy, and performing toilsome journeys to reach them in their mountain homes. As the wife of Dr. Judson, her labors consisted partly in the preparation of books in the Burmese and Peguan languages. Among other things, she translated the first part of "Pilgrim's Progress" into Burmese, and aided in the translation of the New Testament into Peguan.

In 1845 Mrs. Judson's health had became so enfeebled that it was determined to visit America. The voyage was undertaken, but on the 1st of September she died at St. Helena, and was buried on that rocky isle, having labored as a missionary twenty-one years, just half the years of her life.

In October, Dr. Judson arrived with his motherless children at Boston, and during his stay in the United States he did a valuable work for missions. But his heart was in Burmah, whither he felt that he must hasten; Miss Emily Chubbuck, known by her literary productions under the *nom de plume* of "Fanny Forrester," was induced to accompany him as his wife.

Accordingly he returned to Maulmain in the latter part of 1846. Here he finished a Burmese-English dictionary. Three years after his return he was attacked by a severe sickness, and, by advice of friends, undertook a voyage to the Isle of France. His wife's health was at this time in such a condition that she could not accompany him. After the time of his sailing he sank rapidly, and, on the 12th of April, 1850, in the sixty-second year of his age, he fell asleep in Jesus, and was buried in the sea, three days out of sight of the mountains of Burmah. His widow, writing to his sister, thus describes his burial; we make the extract from "The Earnest Man," by Mrs. Conant, to which volume we are chiefly indebted for our sketch:

"They lowered him to his ocean grave without a prayer. His freed spirit had soared above the reach of earthly intercession, and to the foreigners who stood around it would have been a senseless form. And there they left him in his unquiet sepulchre ; but it matters little, for we know that while the unconscious clay is drifting in 'the shifting currents of the restless main,' nothing can disturb the hallowed rest of the immortal spirit. Neither could we have a more fitting monument than the blue waves which visit every coast, for his warm sympathies went forth to the ends of the earth, and included the whole family of man. It is all as God would have it, and our duty is to bend meekly to his will, and wait in faith and patience till we also shall be summoned home."

JOHN NEWTON.

SOME time in the year 1806 a friend said to the parish minister of St. Mary's Woolnoth, London, in view of his extreme age and his many infirmities, "Would it not be well to consider your work of preaching as done?" Instantly the preacher, who was over eighty years old, very deaf, and almost blind, replied, "What! shall the old African blasphemer stop while he can speak?"

John Newton felt that he had been forgiven much, and therefore ought to labor much for Him who had made him a monument of his grace. Even then, when the voice of nature and friends combined to whisper, "Your work of preaching is done," he felt, like the apostle Paul, "Woe is me if I preach not the gospel." He knew that the gospel had saved his soul, and that it could become to others "the wisdom and the power of God unto salvation." He is reported as leaning over his pulpit occasionally, and, with peculiar emphasis, saying, "I never doubted the power of God to save the heathen, since he saved me."

But what a title to give to this aged minister, "The African Blasphemer," even if it came from his own lips! We shall see, as we proceed with our sketch, how he came to deserve it.

John Newton was born near London, in 1725; his father was a sea-captain, and John was left to the care of his mother, who was a devotedly pious woman, and took special pains to impress the truth on the mind of her son. Many years after she was taken home to her rest he wrote concerning her, "Besides the pains my dear mother took with me, she often commended me with many prayers and tears to God, and I doubt not but I reap the fruit of these prayers to this hour."

It was the purpose of Newton's mother to give him to God, and prepare him for the work of the ministry, but her life was spared to him only seven years, her valuable care and instruction being lost to him in that period when he especially needed them. His father soon married again; but John was sent to a boarding-school, where his early religious impressions soon faded away, and he ceased to pray, and learned to curse and blaspheme. At the age of eleven years his father took him with him in his ship, which traded in the Mediterranean, and he continued with his father during five voyages.

John's early impressions were for a time brought back by providential occurrences, such as falling from a horse and narrowly escaping death; the drowning of a companion, with whom he had agreed to go on board a man-of-war, by the upsetting of the boat on which Newton would also have been had he not unexpectedly arrived a few minutes late; but these impressions soon vanished, as the accidents were forgotten. Yet in the midst of his wickedness he was still conscious of a need of God, which often compelled him to offer at least a formal prayer. Finally, an infidel publication fell into his hands, and its ungodly principles operated upon him, as he said, "like a slow poison," and were the occasion of much sorrow.

A short time after this, when John was about seventeen, Captain Newton made an arrangement with a friend to send him to Jamaica, on business which would occupy his attention some years. But before the ship was ready to sail his father despatched him with a message to a place in the neighborhood of Kent. On this visit he met at a friend's house a girl three years younger than himself, for whom he immediately formed a strong and lasting attachment, and who finally became his wife and a valuable helper in the work for which God was preparing him. In consequence of his love for this girl he remained in Kent three weeks, instead of three days, and on his return found that the ship had gone to Jamaica without him. Thus he lost his promised position and incurred the displeasure of his father. He then went as a common sailor in a vessel to Venice, and, aided by the company with whom he associated, made great progress in his downward career. It was at this period that he had a remarkable dream, which he says did much to check him in wickedness. Who can tell but that it was an impression produced on his mind by the Holy Spirit?

"He thought, while walking his watch upon the deck of the ship, a person came to him and gave him a ring, with a charge to keep it faithfully, assuring him that while he kept it he would be happy and prosperous, but if he lost it he would be in trouble and sorrow continually. He accepted it, feeling that there would be no trouble about its being kept by him in safety. A second person came, who, observing the ring on his finger, asked him concerning it, and was told of its virtues, when he laughed at the folly of believing such a statement, and asked him to throw it away. At last he yielded, took it from his finger, and dropped it over the ship's side into the water, when in an instant a terrible fire burst out from a range of mountains; at which his tempter mocked him, and told him that with that ring he had wilfully thrown away the mercy of God. He trembled in great agony, when a third person came to his aid and asked him if he would not act more wisely if the ring were again restored. 'I could,' he says, 'hardly answer, for I thought it gone beyond control. But this friend went down into the water and brought it back, the flames ceased, and the seducer fled. My helper, however, refused to give it to me, lest I should again lose it, but said he would keep it for me and produce it whenever it was needed.'"

This dream, as we have said, produced a lasting impression on his mind, and, for a time, checked him in his downward career.

He was, some time after this, in his nineteenth year, captured by a press-gang and put on board a man-of-war, where his impulsive nature led him into many difficulties, and he meditated suicide; but his love for the girl already spoken of restrained him, and encouraged him to hope for such a position in the future as might enable him to claim her hand. The severity with which he was treated in consequence of a desertion from the ship made it desirable for him to seek a change, as he could not now hope to be befriended by his present captain. He succeeded in exchanging into a vessel bound for Sierra Leone, a popular place for slave-traders. There he abandoned the vessel, and agreed to labor on the Island of Benanoes with a slave-trader. The black woman who acted as this man's wife treated Newton very oppressively; and when he fell sick with a fever he was frequently at the point of death for want of food and water. Yet God preserved him through these troubles, and in his providence rescued him after fifteen months' exposure in this wretched place with more wretched people. It was here that he earned the epithet of the "African blasphemer," and he says of himself, "I know not that I ever met so daring a blasphemer."

But he was not beyond the power of divine grace, and on his way home to England, on board a ship whose captain his father had arranged with to bring him back, he found that "peace of God which passeth all understanding," and which he delighted to preach in after years. The ship was wrecked, and all on board were brought face to face with death. The danger tended to impress the value of a religious hope on his heart. Accordingly, he said, on the 10th of March, 1748, while the ship was kept from sinking by the extraordinary exertion of the crew at the pumps, the Lord sent and delivered him out of deep waters, by the revelation to him of his love and grace.

He arrived at Liverpool in May, 1748, but too late to see his father, who had been appointed governor of York Fort on the western shore of Hudson Bay, and had just started for the place, where in a few years he died. But God had provided Newton another father in the owner of the vessel which brought him home. He soon after returned to Africa as mate on one of his benefactor's vessels. He revisited the scenes of his captivity in Africa, and was again taken sick with fever, and led, when he felt his helplessness, to consecrate himself fully to God. He spent much of his time in studying the Latin language, and afterwards Greek and Hebrew. God was preparing him for his future work, though he knew it not. In 1750 he married Mary Catlett, the lady of whom we have already spoken, and for over forty years she was a loving, faithful help to him in all his work. He took three more voyages, as captain of a slave ship, without conscientious scruples, he says, as to the lawfulness of the trade. Then, in the providence of God, he was led to abandon the sea. In this and many other periods of his history he found it true that "the lot is cast into the lap, but the whole disposing thereof is of the Lord." Frequently, in reviewing the way in which God had led him, he recalled the little incidents on which the course of his life turned, and had no hesitaton in saying, "Here is the hand of God."

In his late years he was accustomed to say that the way of man is not in himself, nor can he conceive what belongs to a single step. "When I go to St. Mary's Woolnoth, it seems the same whether I turn down Lothbury or go through Old Jewry, but the going through one street and not another may produce an effect of lasting consequences. A man cut down my hammock in sport, but had he cut it down half an hour later, I would not have been here, as the exchange of the crew was then making. A man made a smoke on the seashore at the time a ship passed, which was thereby brought to, and afterwards brought me to England."

His own and his father's friend obtained for him, in 1755, the position of tide-surveyor in the port of Liverpool. England was then being stirred by the religious movement inaugurated by Whitefield and the Wesleys. In this movement Newton was much interested, and exercised his gifts, as opportunity offered, in preaching the gospel. His friends urged him to seek ordination from one of the bishops. He applied to the archbishop of York, but his application was refused on the ground of irregularity. Six years later, in 1764, he was presented to the curacy of Olney, in Buckinghamshire, and was ordained deacon by the bishop of Lincoln. He was ordained priest in the following year, the fortieth of his age. Newton formed a warm friendship with Cowper, the poet, doubtless to the comfort and edification of both; and during his residence at Olney he published a volume of hymns, containing several from the pen of Cowper; the others were written by himself. Among the hymns of Newton are the familiar ones beginning—

"Safely through another week."
"'T is a point I long to know."
"Amazing grace! how sweet the sound."
"How sweet the name of Jesus sounds."
"Jesus, who knows full well," etc.

It was during Newton's curacy at Olney that he met Scott, afterwards the well-known commentator, and was the principal means of leading him to the adoption of evangelical views. It was here also that he met that prince of givers, Mr. Thornton, and a friendship began between them which never ended.

Mr. Thornton, after Mr. Newton had proved himself "a workman that needeth not to be ashamed" by sixteen years' labor at Olney, presented him to the living of St. Mary's Woolnoth, London. His first sermon was preached in his new field, December 19, 1779, from the text, "Speaking the truth in love;" and he continued in this charge for twenty-eight years, exemplifying the text in his life. A young man from Scotland attended on Newton's ministry in London, and through his influence was educated at Cambridge, and prepared for his great work as the celebrated Dr. Buchanan, who did so much for missions in India, and whose book on that far-off land determined Judson to go there as a missionary. Thus many waves of influence might be traced back to Newton's faithful, unselfish work for Christ.

Of his numerous writings, his hymns and "Cardiphonia" are best known in the United States. Very many sententious sayings are ascribed to him, which will continue to be used as illustrations while Christianity is preached. Among these are the following:

"If I could go to France and give every man in it a right and peaceable mind by my labor, I should have a statue; but to produce such an effect in the conversion of one soul would be a far greater achievement." "Dr. Taylor of Norwich said to me, 'Sir, I have collated every word in the Hebrew Scriptures seventeen times, and it is very strange if the doctrine of atonement which you hold should not have been found by me.' I am not surprised at this. I once went to light my candle with the extinguisher on it. Now prejudices from education, etc., form an extin-

guisher. It is not enough that you bring the candle; you must remove the extinguisher."
"The heir of a great estate while a child thinks more of a few shillings in his pocket than of his inheritance; so a Christian is often more elated by some frame of heart than by his title to glory."

From his writings we can easily infer that his sermons were full of matter calculated to edify Christians, and to lead sinners to feel the need of the offered Saviour. That such was his purpose is clear from the answer given to a minister who asked his opinion of a sermon that Newton heard him preach. The sermon was a learned, critical disquisition, abounding in nice distinctions. Mr. Newton replied to the inquirer, "When many of your congregation had travelled several miles for a meal, I think you should not have forgotten the important distinction which must ever exist between meat and bones."

Finally, he reached the end of his personal work on earth, trusting to the grace which had already made him so different from what he once was. "If it were not that the Lord is gracious, how could I dare stand before him?" was the expression of his heart as he neared the end of his journey on earth. His only hope was in the death and righteousness of Christ, and in that hope he died, December 21, 1807, after having preached the gospel over forty years. He was buried in the vault of his church, where he had so long proclaimed salvation through the crucified Redeemer. "His works still follow him," and declare that the grace that could thus triumph in the case of the "African blasphemer" can save the very vilest sinner.

WILLIAM MILNE.

IN the beginning of the present century might have been seen a shepherd lad sitting on the brow of a Scottish hill watching his flock, while he read from "The Cloud of Witnesses" of the faithful contending of the martyrs during the persecution under Charles I., and admired their patience, piety, and heroism. He sighed for the time when God would enable him to witness for his name; and that time came when he was far off in the "land of Sinim." He preached, published, taught, and died, that the millions of China might know the love and grace of the Lord Jesus Christ, and thus be led to trust in his name.

William Milne was born in the parish of Kennethmont, Aberdeenshire, in 1785. His father died when he was six years of age. But his father's place was nobly filled by a godly mother, who did what she could to give her son a common school education, and to teach him Willison's Mothers' Catechism, and the Assembly's Shorter Catechism, a thing considered indispensable to the education of the young in that period of Scottish history. But, though the lad had this intellectual knowledge of the doctrines of the Bible, he was a stranger to the power of divine grace. He afterwards wrote, "Religion was very grievous to me in those days," and "I far excelled my equals in profane swearing, and in other sins of a like nature." Yet the Holy Spirit occasionally made his power felt in the boy's heart. Milne records as follows an experience of this kind when he was about ten years old:

"While travelling alone in the middle of the day, between two cornfields, the idea of the eternal punishment of sin in hell struck me with amazing force. My feeling on this occasion exactly corresponded to the language of the prophet, 'Who among us shall dwell with the devouring fire? Who among us shall dwell with everlasting burnings?'"

But even then he did not flee to the refuge set before him in the gospel. A few religious books falling in his way, he was led through their influence to a reformation of life; but as yet he did not feel that he was a ruined sinner, and that if saved at all it must be by a divine Saviour. The Holy Spirit, however, did not leave him, and some years afterwards used the reading of Boston's "Fourfold State," a book then very popular in Scotland, as the means of convincing him of his lost and ruined condition as a sinner. Great was the distress of his mind on his realization of this truth, and he earnestly prayed, as often as ten, and even fifteen times a day, that God would have mercy upon him. Finally, by means of a sermon of Boston's, and of one preached by the pastor of the church which he was in the habit of attending, his distress was removed. The latter sermon was on the text, "And that repentance and remission of sins should be preached in His name among all nations, beginning at Jerusalem." He was led to reason on this wise: "If pardon and salvation were offered without money and without price to those who had killed the Prince of life, and thereby committed the greatest possible crime, then surely that grace which could triumph over all their guilt, and so richly abound where sins of the highest aggravation once abounded, may be extended to me to pardon my sins and renew my nature, to heal and save my soul."

Thus he was led to that Saviour who was not only able, but willing to save just such lost ones as himself. And following the suggestion in the text, "One shall say, I am the Lord's, and another shall call himself by the name of Jacob," etc., he sought a retired place among the hills, where he fed his sheep, and offered himself to God his Saviour "for his service, and to be ruled, sanctified, and saved by him." Soon after he sought to have his name enrolled among God's people, and connected himself with the congregation at Huntly, of which the Rev. G. Cowie was pastor.

Now, having found the Saviour himself, like Andrew and Philip, he began the work of bringing others to Christ. He did not wait until he was commissioned as a missionary to the heathen; but while yet a farm-servant in Scotland he taught in the Sabbath-school, established winter evening prayer-meetings in destitute places in the parish, and visited and prayed with the poor from house to house. Above all, he spent a large portion of his time in secret prayer. And thus he was being prepared for the more difficult work to which the Master was soon to call him.

The congregation to which Milne belonged, under the teaching of its devoted pastor, was far in advance of congregations generally at that period as respects an interest in the heathen; their house of worship was known as "the missionary kirk," and the zeal of their faithful pastor brought upon his head much persecution. It was then thought presumption and an interference with God's plans concerning the heathen to send missionaries to preach to them the way of salvation. But Mr. Milne was soon known around

Huntly as a "mischieve," and when, in the course of time, a friend told him that his brother was thinking of going as a missionary to the heathen—an undertaking then of far greater difficulty, and involving far greater sacrifices, than at the present time—the question at once suggested itself to the mind of Milne, "Can his obligations to the riches of redeeming grace be greater than mine, that he should desire thus to honor God, while I continue satisfied in a state of inglorious ease at home?"

Thus the thought which had impressed itself upon his heart while he was reading "The Cloud of Witnesses" and missionary magazines on the braes, as he watched his sheep, was deepened, and the result was an application to the London missionary society to send him as a missionary. After a careful examination he was accepted, and sent to Gosport to engage in a course of study under the celebrated Dr. Bogus, previous to being assigned to a field of labor. On his way to Gosport he spent a few days in Aberdeen, where he was introduced to the few friends of missions then in that city. Among them was a young lady specially interested in the work, who made him a present of some articles of clothing. The thought never entered the mind of either that the young lady would by-and-by become Mrs. Milne, and be one of the most efficient lady missionaries in China; but so it was. God had chosen her for this work, and in due time would bring it to pass.

Mr. Milne reached Gosport, and made such progress in his studies that in less than two years he was considered well qualified for the work of preaching the gospel to the heathen; and he was accordingly appointed an assistant to Dr. Morrison in China. But though he had pursued his studies at Gosport with zeal and diligence, even there he did not neglect mission work; he often visited and preached to the soldiers in the garrison, and wrote letters to his friends and acquaintances, being successful in leading one of them to follow his example and become a missionary.

The time had now come for Mr. Milne to set out on his journey, which, however, he shrank from undertaking alone, being convinced that a wife would prove both a comfort and a help to him. Strangely enough, a Christian lady in London was the means of introducing him to Miss Cowie, of Aberdeen, the lady to whom we have already alluded. They were married, and embarked for China, September 4, 1812, about seven weeks after his ordination to the work of the ministry. After their arrival at Canton, Mr. Milne wrote his first impressions of China to Dr. Philip, of Aberdeen, as follows:

"This is a vast, benighted country; we stand on the borders of it like men on the bank of the vast sea; we see only a little, and dare venture in but an inch or two. The city of Canton is like the New Jerusalem only in one thing, that strangers are not permitted to enter. A few days ago I went to the top of a hill to view this land (I trust it is a land of promise); my thoughts were, "Oh, that God would give this land to the churches," etc.

Mr. Milne began his study of the language of his mission-field with the same zeal that had characterized him at Gosport, and soon was able to read, translate, and even preach in that strange tongue. After Dr. Morrison had finished the translation of the New Testament into Chinese, it, with a few other small books and tracts, was printed, and Mr. Milne undertook a long journey, chiefly among the neighboring islands, to sell the books, and at the same time preach the gospel. He was also desirous of deciding on some place as a headquarters for the mission work, where schools could be opened without opposition. He at last fixed on Malacca; and thither Mr. and Mrs. Milne removed, and began to lay the foundations for making this the chief station for Chinese mission work. Here they began the work of supplying a Christian literature, and educating the children, hoping by-and-by to supply native preachers for the mainland. Their school was opened August 15, 1815, with five scholars.

Some ten days before this, the first number of a periodical in the Chinese language had been issued, and this, with the Scriptures and tracts, was, as opportunity offered, largely distributed all over China, Cochin China, Siam, and the Malayan Archipelago. Who can tell what a harvest may have been reaped from those first efforts?

In 1817 very convenient mission buildings were completed, including a printing-house and rooms for employés; and an additional periodical in English was commenced. On November 10, 1818, the foundation of the Anglo-Chinese college was laid, and during the year large progress was made in translating the Old Testament into Chinese, the work being divided between Dr. Morrison and Mr. Milne.

In the following March, Mr. Milne was sadly afflicted by the death of his wife, who had in many ways encouraged and helped him in the numerous labors he had undertaken. It was not long, however, that he was left to mourn over his own bereavement and that of his four motherless children, for in the midst of his labors the

Master called for him, June 2, 1822. He had accomplished a great work for China, and now he enjoys the gracious reward which Christ has promised to his faithful servants.

Few men have done more for the cause of Christ in so short a time, for he was a minister of the gospel less than twelve years; but when he came to die, as we learn from Philip's volume, entitled "Life and Opinions of Milne," he repeatedly said "he had no hope of salvation but through the merits of Jesus."

ROBERT POLLOCK.

In the village of Barrhead, Scotland, in the house of the village cabinet-maker, some time in the year 1815, might have been seen standing by the bedside of his loved and loving, but now dying sister, a young lad of seventeen summers, with thoughtful countenance and sympathetic heart. It was not the first time that he had been called to witness the contest with the king of terrors: some ten years previous to this, a loved brother of tender years had been taken from his side, and for a whole day nothing could dry the tears which his grief had produced; and now, we have no doubt, busy memory was bringing up before him images of the former sad parting, and suggesting thought concerning the unseen world, whose portals his sister was so near.

The loved one passed away, and Robert Pollock, some years later, expressed his feelings at her loss in tenderest poetry. It was at the close of a period renowned in British history for some of the noblest poetical productions. The strains of Cowper, Coleridge, Crabbe, Campbell, Byron, and Burns were vibrating in the ears of the people, and it seemed like temerity in the extreme for a new poet to seek to win attention, unless possessed of extraordinary gifts. It is probable that Pollock little questioned what reception would be given him, but instinctively gave utterance to his love and sympathy in harmonions lines. Two years afterwards, when he projected and wrote "The Course of Time," he gave the lines suggested by his sister's death a place in the fifth book of the poem.

We give the following extract. It not only shows how Christians can die, but holds up before us some of the blessed hopes which sustain their souls as they pass through the shaded valley.

"I do remember, and will ne'er forget,
The dying eye; that eye alone was bright,
And brighter grew as nearer death approached:
As I have seen the gentle little flower
Look fairest in the silver beam which fell
Reflected from the thunder cloud, that soon
Came down, and o'er the desert scattered far
And wide its loveliness. She made a sign
To bring her babe. 'Twas brought, and by her placed.
She looked upon its face—that neither smiled,
Nor wept, nor knew who gazed upon't—and laid
Her hand upon its little breast and sought
For it, with look that seemed to penetrate
The heavens, unutterable blessings, such
As God to dying parents only granted
For infants left behind them in the world.
'God keep my child!' we heard her say, and heard
No more: the angel of the covenant

> Was come, and, faithful to his promise, stood
> Prepared to walk with her through death's dark vale.
> And now her eyes grew bright, and brighter still,
> Too bright for ours to look upon, suffused
> With many tears—and closed without a cloud.
> They set as sets the morning star, which goes
> Not down behind the darkened west, nor hides
> Obscured among the temples of the sky,
> But melts away into the light of heaven."

What effect this dying scene had upon the youth's susceptible mind we cannot tell. It may be that this patient, trustful departure of his beloved sister was the lesson sent by God to impress upon his mind earth's vanities and heaven's verities—the light that should so shine upon *him*, that, like Saul, he would say, "Lord, what wilt thou have me to do?" At any rate, he very soon after could say, "Woe is unto me if I preach not the gospel."

His determination being heartily approved by his godly parents, measures were at once taken to secure the education necessary to fit him to enter upon the responsible work of his calling. He engaged with zeal in his preparatory studies, encouraged, as well he might be, by the glorious rewards which every faithful minister of Christ may hope to obtain, and which he himself afterwards so well described, in a missionary address, as follows:

"But were I to say that the present contemplation of the victorious march of truth in the lands of ignorance was all the reward which awaits the Christian's exertions, I should be speaking apart from the words of inspiration. When this world, with all its enjoyments, has passed away, when gold cannot purchase one luxurious dish to the voluptuary, nor one moment's repose to the careless, nor one grim smile to the earth-grasping miser, then shall the exertions of the Christian receive their full reward. When that Christian who has been the means of spiritually enlightening the mind of a fellow-creature has 'put on immortality,' when he is reposing himself on the ever-verdant banks of the river of life, then from him shall be heard a louder note of praise swelling the eternal hosannas of heaven. How much will it add to his endless bliss to shake hands, in the regions of immortality, with some once inhabitant of the desert, whom he has been permitted, by his benefactions, to be the means of elevating from the wastes of darkness, suffering, and death, and of placing amid the brightness of immortal day and the felicities of eternal life. His services have been great, and his reward shall be in proportion to his services. 'The liberal soul shall be made fat; and he that watereth shall be watered also himself.' 'They that be wise (or, teachers) shall shine as the brightness of the firmament; and they that turn many to righteousness, as the stars for ever and ever.' Verily, all who serve Christ shall find that his 'reward is with him.'"

Having finished his preparatory studies, Pollock entered the University of Glasgow, in 1817, at a period when that celebrated seat of learning was more than usually favored with efficient professors. Professors Mylne and Young seem to have been the young man's favorites. In regard to the first, Pollock wrote to his brother: "In Mr. Mylne's class I was set free for ever from the trammels of book authority;" and in his note-book he styled the second "a wonderful man."

During the period of his studies in college Pollock indulged himself freely in writing both prose and poetry—fugitive pieces, however. It had not yet entered into his mind to produce a volume. Among these pieces his ode entitled "The Distressed Christian to his Soul" is worthy of notice. It is said to be his second effort at blank verse. How just and animating is the thought of the following extract:

"No, no, my soul! life and eternal joy,
A crown of glory, an unfading crown,
Imparted from the grandeur infinite
Of glory uncreated, will be thine,
If in the path of duty thou abide.

That God who into being spoke the world,
And still with arm omnipotent maintains
The revolution vast of varied things,
Hath sworn by his eternal Godhead high
That he who perseveres in righteousness,
Who fights the fight of faith, and turns not back,
Shall immortality and honor gain;
Unseen, unheard, unthought of happiness;
Bliss which Jehovah's goodness has prepared.

"Rise, rise, my soul; see yonder blest abode;
Behold the beatific vision bright;
And say how ill it fits thee e'er to fret,
Or be dismayed at Time's most horrid frown.
Put on the Christian armor; bravely fight
The hosts of earth and hell; fear not their strength;
Power, wisdom infinite, are on thy side.
The mighty Arm that clave Arabia's gulf,
Whelmed Egypt's guilty host infuriate,
Uplifted, fights for thee. Away, away,
Ye bugbears that surround my soul! Earth, death
And hell are foiled by Him in whom resides
All strength. Eternal victory is thine,
Immortal life, and everlasting bliss."

During the same period he read, in one of the college societies, a remarkable essay on "Originality," his purpose being to show that there may be as much originality in the use of old figures as in the invention of new ones.

Pollock did not, however, waste his time in scribbling, but gave such attention to his studies as enabled him to stand high in his classes, and to benefit from the instructions of his professors. This is evident from the fact that, at the close of the logic class, he obtained the prize offered for the best essay on the "External Senses."

His college course being finished in the fall of 1822, he entered the Divinity Hall, or theological seminary, of the United Secession, now the United Presbyterian Church. In addition to the usual studies prescribed in the course, he read critically the standard English poets. Milton was his favorite; and about this time he records a singular dream in which he holds conversation with that poet, a conception readily explained by his frequent study of his works.

During his studies his pecuniary necessities compelled him to seek relief by the labor of his pen; accordingly he wrote, in one week, "Helen of the Glen," a Sunday-school book still popular among the young, for which he received from a Glasgow publisher fifteen pounds. Subsequently, for the same reason, he wrote two other volumes, "The Persecuted Family," and "Ralph Gemmell," which are still in demand by the reading public. During his studies in the seminary he made an address on preaching, before a students' society, which is still worthy of the attention of theological students.

While pursuing his studies in Divinity Hall, one night in December, 1824, he took from his table "Hartley's Oratory," a collection of prose and verse, and turned to Byron's "Darkness." While reading this, the idea of a poem on the resurrection suggested itself to his mind; and at once he seized a pen and wrote the following, now forming part of Book 7 of "The Course of Time:"

> "In 'customed glory bright that morn the sun
> Rose, visiting the earth with light and heat
> And joy, and seemed as full of youth, and strong
> To mount the steep of heaven, as when the stars
> Of morning sang to his first dawn, and night
> Fled from his face. The spacious sky received
> Him blushing, as a bride when on her looked
> The bridegroom; and spread out beneath his eyes
> Earth smiled. Up to his warm embrace the dews,
> That all night long had wept his absence, flew;
> The herbs and flowers their fragrant stores unlocked,
> And gave the wanton breeze—that, newly woke,
> Revelled in sweets, and from its wings shook health—
> A thousand grateful smells; the joyous woods
> Dried in his beams their locks, wet with the drops
> Of night; and all the sons of music sung
> Their matin song."

With this plan before him, in several successive weeks he wrote as much as a thousand lines. During a visit to his home at Moorhouse to see his mother, who was dying of consumption, he was sitting alone one night, meditating, it is probable, on the life, death, and future of this loved mother, when the conception of the "Course of Time" burst upon his mind, and made such an impression upon him that he shook with excitement. This new plan required new chapters and more extensive research and labor. Yet in nineteen months he completed the whole, writing in the last five weeks thirty-five hundred lines.

The plot of the poem is simple. It is the Scripture history of man, the plan of redemption, and the judgment. The story is told by a redeemed earth bard to "two beautiful sons of Paradise" and a stranger who had asked them, as they gazed from the battlements of heaven, concerning a fearful place which he had seen, as with swift wing he swept through space from his native place to heaven. He described the place as follows:

> "And deep as wide, and ruinous as deep,
> Beneath I saw a lake of burning fire
> With tempest tossed perpetually, and still
> The waves of fiery darkness 'gainst the rocks
> Of dark damnation broke, and music made
> Of melancholy sort; and overhead,
> And all around, wind warred with wind, storm howled
> To storm, and lightning forked lightnings crossed,
> And thunder answered thunder, muttering sounds
> Of sullen wrath," etc.

The "youthful sons" could not answer his inquiry, but invited him to go with them to the

> "Ancient bard of earth,
> Who, by the stream of life sitting in bliss,
> Has oft beheld the eternal years complete

The mighty circle round the throne of God;
Great in all learning, in all wisdom great,
And great in song; whose harp in lofty strain
Tells frequently of what thy wonder craves."

He accompanies them, and receives from their bard the answer that the place beheld was hell, the region of the lost. And that he may understand who dwell there, and why they came there, the bard tells him of creation, the plan of redemption, man's character, and the final judgment. In the narrative there are many episodes, and great facility is shown in describing the virtues, vices, and employments of men, as well as their principles and hopes. We can give only two extracts—the first being part of an encomium on the Bible. The seer asks,

"Hast thou ever heard
Of such a book? The author God himself,
The subject God and man, salvation, life,
And death, eternal life, eternal death.
Dread words! whose meaning has no end, no bounds.
Most wondrous book! Bright candle of the Lord!
Star of eternity! The only star
By which the barque of man could navigate
The sea of life, and gain the coast of bliss
Securely! Only star which rose on Time,
And on its dark and troubled billows—still
As generation, drifting swiftly by,
Succeeded generation—threw a ray
Of heaven's own light, and to the hills of God,
The eternal hills, pointed the sinner's eye.
By prophets, seers, and priests, and sacred bards,

Evangelists, apostles, men inspired
And by the Holy Ghost anointed, set
Apart and consecrated to declare
To earth the counsels of the Eternal One,
This book, this holiest, this sublimest book,
Was sent. Heaven's will, Heaven's code of laws entire
To man, this book contained: defined the bounds
Of vice and virtue, and of life and death,
And what was shadow, what was substance, taught."

Our second extract is part of the well-known description of Byron:

"He touched his harp, and nations heard entranced.
As some vast river of unfailing source,
Rapid, exhaustless, deep, his numbers flowed,
And oped new fountains in the human heart.
Where Fancy halted, weary in her flight,
In other men, his, fresh as morning, rose,
And soared untrodden heights, and seemed at home
Where angels bashful looked.
. . . .
Great man! the nations gazed and wondered much,
And praised; and many called his evil good.
Wits wrote in favor of his wickedness,
And kings to do him honor took delight.
Thus full of titles, flattery, honor, fame,
Beyond desire, beyond ambition full,
He died. He died of what? Of wretchedness:
Drank every cup of joy, heard every trump
Of fame; drank early, deeply drank; drank draughts
That common millions might have quenched; then died
Of thirst, because there was no more to drink.
. . . .
His groanings filled the land his numbers filled;
And yet he seemed ashamed to groan, poor man!
Ashamed to ask; and yet he needed help.

> Proof, this, beyond all lingering of doubt,
> That not with natural or mental wealth
> Was God delighted, or his peace secured;
> That not in natural or mental wealth
> Was human happiness or grandeur found.
> Attempt how monstrous, and how surely vain,
> With things of earthly sort, with aught but God,
> With aught but moral excellence, truth, and love,
> To satisfy and fill the immortal soul.
> Attempt vain inconceivably! Attempt
> To satisfy the ocean with a drop,
> To marry Immortality to Death;
> And with the unsubstantial shade of Time
> To fill the embrace of all Eternity!"

"The poem," says the biographer of Pollock, "shone forth like a comet on the literary circles of Edinburgh and London, and soon became the absorbing topic of conversation. The harp of Scotland had suddenly been struck by a master-hand to notes of holy minstrelsy. . . . . It took its place like a planet of the largest class among the other members in the firmament of song, and its brilliancy has increased with every succeeding year."

The poem being finished, Pollock gave himself still more arduously to his studies, preparatory to engaging in the work of the ministry; and finally, in May, 1827, he was licensed to preach from the pulpit the gospel which he had already proclaimed in his great poem. But his work was nearly ended; the messenger of death was close behind him; and although his poetical achievement had secured to him numerous friends, able and willing to help him as far as human skill and wealth could do it, yet all were in vain. On September 15, 1827, the same year in which his poem was published, and his first sermon preached, in the twenty-ninth year of his age, the Master took him to "the courts above," to sing still more sweetly than he had done on earth. His friends erected over his grave a monument with the following inscription: "The grave of Robert Pollock, author of 'The Course of Time.' His immortal poem is his monument." And, we may add, through it, though dead, he still preaches the glorious gospel of the blessed Saviour.

THOMAS CHALMERS.

THOMAS CHALMERS was born in a small town in Fifeshire, Scotland, on the 17th of March, 1780. His parents were noted for their decision of character and piety. John Chalmers, his father, occupied a leading position among his fellow-townsmen of Anstruther, and at one time filled the office of provost of the town. He was also in a position to experience the truth of the declaration, "Happy is the man that hath his quiver full of them (children); they shall not be ashamed, but they shall speak with the enemies in the gate." He had fourteen children, of whom Thomas was the sixth. At the early age of three years Thomas was sent to school; he, however, manifested no special fondness for study, but was rather distinguished for his love of the sports of the playground. Yet he soon learned to read, and found delight in "The Pilgrim's Progress" and the narratives of Scripture. Fifty years afterwards he said of such reading, "I feel quite sure that the use of the sacred dialogues as a school-book, and the pictures of Scripture scenes which interested my boyhood, still cling to me, and impart a peculiar tinge and charm to the same representations when brought within my notice." He manifested intense sympathy, even in his earliest years, with the sufferings of humanity. Having heard his father read the story of Absalom's rebellion and death, he was afterwards found in the nursery, much excited, repeating the words, "Oh, my son Absalom! O Absalom, my son, my son!"

He early determined to become a minister of the gospel, and chose for his first text, "Let brotherly love continue." His affectionate, warm-hearted nature could not but appreciate the doctrine of such a text, and it was dear to him as long as he lived. His motto was, Where organic union cannot be obtained, let there be coöperation among Christians of every name.

At the age of twelve he was sent to the University of St. Andrews; he was too young to fully appreciate its privileges, and for two years he made little progress. In his fourteenth year, however, he entered on the study of mathematics, under Prof. Dr. James Brown, when his mind was aroused from its lethargy and first began to manifest its vast power. Mathematical study had special attraction for him, and he never lost his relish for it, and ever afterwards regarded it as one of the best instrumentalities for training the mind.

The French Revolution was in progress at this time, and even Scotland was not free from the excitement of that sad period in French history. Prof. Brown sympathized with many of the principles of the radical school of politics, and Chalmers warmly embraced his sentiments, and is said to have read "Goodwin's Political Justice" with delight and approval. The excitement and the discussion of the times did much to loosen his hold on the conservative principles that he had been taught in his home at Anstruther; but after a while he was led back again to the true conservatism and the holy religion which he had seen exemplified in the house of his father.

In 1795, when not yet sixteen years of age, he was enrolled as a student of theology, and, though by no means prepared to study it, because not yet enlightened by the Spirit of God, he nevertheless made great progress in formalism, and it is said that when his turn came to lead in prayer in the public hall, many of the citizens crowded to hear him. So nearly may the formalist copy the true Christian.

Towards the close of his first year in the theological hall, a new era was opened up in his mental life by the study of "Edwards on the Will." This work was to him a source of intense pleasure, and a mine which furnished to him treasures of the profoundest thought. He was spellbound by the clear reasoning of the treatise, and filled with awe by the majesty of its doctrine. His mind expanded and became ennobled as he thought of infinite wisdom guiding and controlling the destinies of the sons of men. Twenty-four years afterwards he wrote, "I remember, when a student of divinity, and long ere I could relish evangelical sentiment, I spent nearly a twelvemonth in a sort of mental elysium, and the one idea which ministered to my soul all its rapture was the magnificence of the Godhead, and the universal subordination of all things to the one great purpose for which he evolved and was supporting creation. I should like to be so inspired over again, but with such a view of the Deity as coalesced and was in harmony with the doctrine of the New Testament."

During the last year of his theological course, as he was required to attend lectures only three months, he engaged as a tutor in a private family. In this position he was treated in a haughty and scornful manner by his employers, a thing to which his independent mind could not well submit. Accordingly, after six months' service, he relinquished his position, making the following reply to his employer, when taunted by him with being proud: "There are," said he, "two kinds of pride, sir: there is that pride which lords it over inferiors; and there is that pride which rejoices in repressing the insolence of superiors. The first I have none of; the second I glory in." Yet with all the independence of character which Chalmers evidenced in his intercourse with his fellow-men, he was, after he found the Saviour, characterized by the humility and trustfulness of a little child when he drew near to God. So the apostle Paul in all sincerity could declare, "I am less than the least of all the saints," and also, "I suppose I was not a whit behind the very chiefest apostles. But though I be rude in speech, yet not in knowledge."

Having become dissatisfied with the work of a tutor, Chalmers applied, after finishing his course at the theological hall, for licensure; and after some difficulty, on account of his age—he being only nineteen years old, and the rule requiring students to be twenty-one before they are taken on trial for licensure—he was licensed, July 31, 1779, to preach the gospel of the grace of God, on the plea that "he was a lad of pregnant parts."

After his licensure he attended lectures in Edinburgh during two winters, and was much interested, and no doubt profited by the prelections of Drs. Stewart and Robinson. About this time, through the influence of a former classmate, he was appointed assistant to the parish minister at

Cavers, in Roxburghshire; but he was not satisfied with this position. It was the height of his ambition to obtain a professorship in one of the colleges of his native country, and he sought whatever might tend to the consummation desired. Accordingly, he applied for and obtained the position of assistant to the mathematical professor in St. Andrews University, and soon after was appointed pastor of Kilmany, a parish some nine miles distant from St. Andrews, and was ordained and settled in this parish in May, 1803. His success as a teacher aroused the opposition of the incumbent of the mathematical chair in the university, and Chalmers was dismissed from his position at the end of the term. He keenly felt this treatment as a blow at his reputation, and determined to compete single-handed with the university in the following winter, which he did with success, drawing from the college a large number of students to his mathematical and chemistry classes.

A few years afterwards, in 1808, he published his first book, an "Inquiry into the Extent and Stability of National Resources," a work called forth by the national alarm at Napoleon's decrees against British commerce. The publication of this book helped to make the author's reputation. He was soon after elected delegate to the General

Assembly, and made a notable speech, which at once brought him into prominence in the church, showing the need of adequate salaries for the ministers, in order to an increase of their influence and usefulness.

Chalmers now gloried in the church and in Christianity as a system of truth. To quote his own words, "I revere Christianity, not because it is the religion of my fathers; I revere it not because it is the established religion of my country; I revere it not because it brings to me the emoluments of office; but I revere it because it is built upon the solid foundation of impregnable arguments; because it has improved the world by the lessons of an ennobling morality." After a little while he was able to add: because of its power to make wise unto salvation; because it revealed a Saviour able and willing to save lost and ruined man. That Saviour he had not yet found. For some seven years, at Kilmany, he preached a theoretical religion; he could expatiate with eloquent tongue "on the meanness of dishonesty, on the villany of falsehood, on the despicable arts of calumny;" but the thief would still steal, and the liar would still utter his falsehoods. To minister to the repression of wickedness in the listeners, there was needed a new nature in the preacher; but that new nature could be found only by coming to that Saviour whom he had not yet embraced.

But he was laid upon a bed of sickness; brothers and sisters were taken away; and the Holy Sprit was at work impressing upon his heart the need of a better righteousness than his own. Wilberforce's "Practical View of Religion," Scott's "Force of Truth," and Hannah More's "Essay on Practical Piety" also contributed to enlighten his darkness and enable him to see the suitability of the Saviour to meet his wants; and in 1810 his style of preaching changed entirely. Instead of preaching to uninterested hearers a cold morality, he soon had a crowded assembly of anxious listeners, as from a full heart he addressed them in such words as, "It is not because you are so great a sinner that I would have you to be comforted, but because Jesus Christ is so great a Saviour; it is not the smallness of sin, but the greatness of him who died for it. I would have you to be satisfied, but not with self. . . . . I would have you listen to that loud and widely-sounding call, 'Look unto me, and be ye saved, all ye ends of the earth.'" And as an illustration of the effect of such sermons, his biographer gives the following facts: "In the spring of 1812 he preached on the text, 'God so loved the world,' etc., John 3: 16. Two young men, Alexander

Patterson and Robert Eddie, heard the discourse, and as they journeyed homeward one asked the other, 'Did you feel anything particularly in church to-day?' The other replied, 'I never felt myself to be a lost sinner until to-day, when I was listening to that sermon.' 'It is very strange,' rejoined the other, 'it was just the same with me.' They turned from their path into a neck of woods, and, screened by the foliage, they together knelt and prayed. Both dated their conversion from that day. Alexander Patterson afterwards became the celebrated missionary among the lanes and by-ways of Edinburgh, and the other was active in every form of Christian usefulness."

In 1813 an article on Christianity which Chalmers had for some years been engaged upon, and whose preparation had contributed to the spiritual change which he had experienced, appeared in the Edinburgh Encyclopædia, and was republished separately, with additions, under the title of "Evidences of Christianity."

The fame of the wonderful preacher spread over Scotland, and soon a deputation from the Town Council of Glasgow came to hear him; he was invited to become pastor of the Tron Church of that city, and left Kilmany in July, 1815. At Glasgow he delivered his celebrated astronomical discourses, which were published in January,

1817, and within the year nine editions were called for. Never before did a volume of sermons meet with such a demand; nearly twenty thousand copies were sold within the year. It was during this year, when he was at the very height of his popularity, that he visited London to preach the anniversary sermon of the London Missionary Society, in Surrey Chapel; and although the service did not begin until eleven o'clock, the chapel was crowded at seven o'clock in the morning. Concerning this sermon, which was from the singular text, 1 Cor. 14:22-25, Mr. Smith, the publisher, wrote, "I write under the nervousness of having heard and witnessed the most astonishing display of human talent that, perhaps, ever commanded sight or hearing. . . . Nothing from the Tron pulpit ever exceeded it."

As a matter of course, so able and popular a preacher was sought by other communities wherever it was thought that it was possible to obtain him; accordingly, Stirling and Edinburgh parishes sought his services, but were refused; but he accepted a call to St. John's, a new parish in Glasgow, where he thought he could carry out more fully his peculiar views of caring for the whole people of the parish by means of church officers. He was assisted in his work by the afterwards celebrated Edward Irving.

Notwithstanding the success of Chalmers as a preacher and pastor, he had still some love for professorial work, the remains of his first ambition, and he accepted an appointment to the chair of Moral Philosophy at St. Andrews, in 1823. A few years afterwards, in 1828, he was transferred to the chair of Theology in Edinburgh University. In this position he remained until the disruption, or withdrawal of a large body of clergymen and laymen from the established church of Scotland, in 1843, when he was elected to the chair of Theology in the new college founded by the newly-formed "Free Church." During his professorship of some fifteen years in the University of Edinburgh, he abounded in labors having for their object both the temporal and spiritual welfare of men. He was the leading spirit in the controversies which resulted in the formation of the Free Church, which claimed for congregations a voice in the selection of their pastors; and more than any other he provided for that church the compact organization which has since done so much to make it a power, not only in Scotland, but in the world.

During the four years which he lived after the disruption, he was instant in season and out of season, that he might promote the cause of the divine Redeemer. And if he loved and labored for the Free Church, it was because he thought he could thereby best subserve the object for which the church was instituted by its divine Head. Our space does not permit us to notice his literary labors, his efforts in behalf of education, and his missionary work in West Port, Edinburgh, among the most degraded of that city's population. His biographer says, "The physical and moral condition of this community was deplorable; one-fourth were paupers on the poor roll, one-fourth were street beggars, thieves, or prostitutes." But even among these "the gospel was the power of God unto salvation." They were the possessors of souls worth more than the entire world, and Dr. Chalmers, with all his mighty intellect, did not think it a waste of time to proclaim to them that Saviour who "is able to save to the uttermost all that come unto God by him."

But his work on earth was nearly finished. His last sermon was preached from the text, Isa. 27:4, 5, and on Monday morning, May 31, 1847, he was found dead in his bed, having passed away apparently without any struggle. On June 4 he was carried to his grave. Concerning the immense numbers that formed his funeral procession, composed of all classes, the high and the low, the rich and the poor alike, a spectator at the time wrote: "There was a moral sublimity in the spectacle. It spoke more emphatically than by words of the dignity of intrinsic excellence, and of the height to which a true man may attain. It was the dust of a Presbyterian minister which the coffin contained, and yet they were burying him amid the tears of a nation, and with more than kingly honors."

JOHN WILLIAMS.

In the Island of Rarotonga, at Arorangi, a large stone monument stands, with the following inscription, in English and in Rarotongan: "To the memory of Rev. John Williams, of the London Missionary Society, who, having labored upwards of fourteen years at Raiatea, was made the honored instrument of introducing Christianity to the Hervey and Samoan Islands. In attempting to convey the gospel to the New Hebrides, he fell a sacrifice, with his friend Mr. Harris, on the island of Erromango, to the cruelty of the deluded heathen inhabitants, November 20, 1839."

Yes, on that sad day, over forty years ago, the club of a cannibal ended the life and self-denying labor of one of England's noblest missionaries.

John Williams was born June 20, 1796, at Tottenham, a suburb of London. His mother, previous to her marriage, was an attendant on the ministry of the Rev. William Romaine, and, although not converted to Christ until after her removal from London, it is believed that the truths which she heard from that earnest man were the means of shaping her principles, and, finally, of determining the character of her son, John Williams.

When he arrived at proper age he was apprenticed to an ironmonger in City Road, London, a circumstance which did not appear very favorable to his accomplishment of any great work in the world, but which he afterwards found was intended, in the providence of God, as one preparation for the great task designed for him. Here he had an opportunity of gaining that mechanical knowledge and skill which were afterwards of immense value to him in his work among the islands of the sea. But while he was making progress in the direction of his trade, he was not improving equally fast in moral and spiritual qualifications. One Sabbath evening in 1814, when he was in his eighteenth year, he made arrangements to meet some of his godless companions, and to go with them to a tea-garden. While waiting on the street for them, and feeling a little angry because they were behind time, the wife of his employer passed along and asked him to accompany her to church. He unwillingly yielded, and went with her to the Tabernacle, where Rev. Timothy East, of Birmingham, preached a sermon on Matt. 16 : 26: "What is a man profited if he shall gain the whole world, and lose his own soul? or what shall a man give in exchange for his soul?" The Spirit of God applied the truth spoken to his heart; he became a new man, and new motives controlled his life.

Twenty-four years afterwards, when his name was known not only in the South Sea Islands, but everywhere throughout Great Britain, he stood in that same pulpit, and said, "I have the door in my view at which I then entered; and I have all the circumstances of that important era in my history vividly impressed upon my mind; and I have in my eye at this instant the particular spot on which I took my seat; I have, also, a distinct impression of the powerful sermon that was that evening preached by the excellent Mr. East; and God was pleased, in his gracious providence, to influence my mind at that time so powerfully that I forsook all my worldly companions."

He soon after connected himself with the congregation, and engaged with zeal in the Christian work undertaken by it. In the year 1815, in consequence of information given through the auxiliary mission society of this congregation concerning the state of the heathen, Mr. Williams became deeply impressed with the conviction that it was his duty to become a missionary. This feeling was fostered by his pastor, the Rev. Matthew Wilks; and, finally, Mr. Williams, after having passed the usual examination, was accepted as a missionary by the London Missionary Society, July, 1816, and appointed to the South Sea Islands, while others were to go to Africa. In October he was married to an estimable lady, who was ever a helpmeet in his work, Miss Mary Chauner, a member of the Tabernacle congregation.

It was finally determined that the missionaries should sail November 17, 1816; among them was the afterwards celebrated Robert Moffat. In May, 1817, the vessel reached Sydney, where Mr. Williams remained, laboring as he best could, until September 4, when a vessel was found to take him to Tahiti, where he landed on the 17th of November, a whole year after he had left London. The difficulties of access to any field of missionary labor have now been in great part removed, and weeks, instead of months, measure the time of travel.

Among the first things that Mr. Williams engaged in at the place of his residence, Eimeo, an island near Tahiti, was to aid in building a vessel, that some means of communication with other islands might be had. Missionaries had been laboring with success at Eimeo for about five years; it was therefore thought best to extend the work to other islands; and finally Mr. Williams embarked for Raiatea, after visiting Huaheine. Raiatea is the largest and most lofty of the western group of the Society Islands. Some of its mountains rise two thousand feet above the level of the sea, and it is naturally a lovely island. But in 1818 the usages of its people were most debasing and cruel, and their island was "the focus and source of the abominable idolatries which had darkened and destroyed the inhabitants of its own and surrounding shores." But scarcely two years rolled around before the people of this island formed themselves into a missionary society to send the gospel to others. At their first meeting King Tamatoa presided, and addressed the large assembly thus:

"Remember what you used to do for your lying gods. You used to give them all your time, your strength, your property, and even your lives. Then you had nothing of your own; it was all the evil spirit's. . . . . But now all your property is your own, and here are your teachers; God sent them. . . . . Now your eyes are open, and you see it is all false, all *paranpoke*—word and work which end in death. Let us do what we learn; let us take pity upon other lands ; let us give property willingly, with our whole heart, to send them missionaries." And they did give willingly and liberally, for their contributions of cocoanut oil brought the society that year $2,500.

Mr. Williams having, by the blessing of God,

accomplished so much for Raiatea, now turned his thought to other islands, and in October, 1821, he sailed for Aitutaki, one of the Hervey or Cook group. Leaving teachers there, he sailed to Sydney, where he purchased a vessel for Raiatea, that the inhabitants might have the means of transporting their produce, which was now fast increasing. The religion of Christ blesses men in time, as well as prepares them for eternity. Mr. Williams fully believed in this doctrine, and used his influence everywhere to promote the civil, as well as the moral and spiritual welfare of the people among whom he labored.

Soon after his return to Raiatea he, with six native teachers, undertook another voyage to Aitutaki in the new vessel, which he named "The Endeavor." At Aitutaki he met some natives of Rarotonga, an island not then on the map. Mr. Williams set out to discover it, and, succeeding after several attempts, found it the finest and most populous island of the Hervey group. The results of his discovery are well told by the monument to which we have already alluded. His first visit to Rarotonga was made in 1823, and two years afterwards he wrote from there, "Our men have brought us the most pleasing news, with ocular demonstration, of the triumphs of the mighty gospel. All idolatry is abolished in this populous island. They have erected a chapel one hundred and six fathoms in length. Perhaps you may say I have made a mistake, but I have not. It is upwards of six hundred feet long, and all the people cannot get into it." So rapid and thorough a change shows how admirably fitted the religion of Christ is to reach down to and lift up the most degraded of our race. It was on this island that Mr. Williams afterwards built the "Messenger of Peace," which he used so efficiently in introducing the gospel to other islands. While he was engaged in this undertaking, his mechanical genius and the acquirements of his apprenticeship came to his aid, and enabled him to make the tools necessary for constructing the vessel; and in fifteen weeks he completed and launched a boat sixty feet long and eighteen feet wide. With this vessel, which he could call his own, he made many voyages, introducing Christian native preachers in many islands, visiting and encouraging those already at work, and aiding them in contending against the difficulties which they were called on to meet, not the least of which was the introduction, by trading ships, of ardent spirits. When will this curse be banished from every Christian land? And when will civilized and nominally Christian nations cease to impose it upon barbarous and heathen peoples?

JOHN WILLIAMS. 249

Finally, Mr. Williams determined to visit his native land, and arrived there in June, 1834, after an absence of eighteen years.

He was received in England by all classes with much enthusiasm, and became at once exceedingly popular as a speaker through the power with which he advocated the cause of missions, so that the churches could scarcely hold the people who assembled to hear him. By his sermons, addresses, and the volume which he wrote and published at this period, his "Narrative of Missionary Enterprises in the South Sea Islands," which was extensively circulated, he awakened a new interest in the mission work among all classes, both in England and Scotland.

At the annual meeting of the missionary society, in 1835, he spoke warmly in favor of increasing the work, and of an effort to induce the various denominations to divide heathendom among them, and thus cover the whole earth with the glad news of salvation.

During this visit to England he superintended the publication of the New Testament in Rarotongan, having completed the translation before leaving the South Sea Islands.

Having spent nearly four years in his work of lecturing and publishing, Mr. Williams began to think of returning to his field of labor. But it was necessary first to obtain a vessel more suited to his wants than the one which he had built himself; and, after failing in obtaining one from the government, to which he applied on the ground of the value of the mission work to the commerce of the country, he collected from friends of missions nearly twenty thousand dollars, with which he bought and equipped the "Camden," a vessel admirably adapted to his purpose. On this he embarked for his field of labor in April, 1838, taking with him sixteen other missionaries, assigned to various islands.

Mr. Williams took up his residence in the Samoan group, and labored there when not visiting and locating teachers on the other islands. In November, 1839, he undertook his last voyage of visitation. Just before he embarked on the Camden a blind chief visited him, and said,

"Teacher Williams, I am a blind man, but I have a great desire to go with you to the dark lands. Perhaps my being blind will make the people pity me and not kill me; and while I can talk to them and tell them about Jesus, my boy [placing his hand on the head of his son] can read and write, and so we can teach these things." How changed was this chief from his former cruel and bloodthirsty self!

Next day, November 4, 1839, the Camden

sailed, with Mr. Williams and several native teachers, who were to be left at the islands that were willing to receive them. Having left three of these teachers at the Island of Tanna, the vessel proceeded to Erromango, where, on the morning of the 20th of November, Mr. Williams and his friend Mr. Harris landed, and were slain by the clubs of the natives. Capt. Morgan, the commander of the Camden, gives the following description of the scene, quoted in the "Life of Mr. Williams" by Ebenezer Prout.

"Mr. Williams remarked that he saw a number of boys playing, and thought it a good sign as implying that the natives had no bad intentions. I said I thought so too, but I would rather see some women also, because when the natives resolve on mischief they send the women out of the way; there were no women on the beach. At last he got up, went forward in the boat, and landed. He presented his hand to the natives, which they were unwilling to take. He then called to me to hand some cloth out of the boat, and he sat down and divided it among them, endeavoring to win their confidence. All three walked up the beach, Mr. Harris first, Mr. Williams and Mr. Cunningham following. After they had walked about one hundred yards, they turned to the right, alongside of the bush, and I lost sight of them; Mr. Harris was the farthest off. I then went on shore, supposing that we had found favor in the eyes of the people. I stopped to see the boat anchored safely, and then walked up the beach towards the spot where the others had proceeded, but before I had gone one hundred yards the boat's crew cried out to me to run to the boat. I looked round, and saw Mr. Williams and Mr. Cunningham running, Mr. Cunningham towards the boat and Mr. Williams towards the sea, with one native close behind him. I got into the boat, and by this time two natives were close behind me, though I did not see them at the moment. By this time Mr. Williams had got to the water, but the beach being stony and steep, he fell backward, and the native struck him with a club, and often repeated the blow. A short time after another native came up and struck him, and very soon another came up and pierced several arrows into his body," which was afterwards nearly consumed by the cannibalistic savages.

But, though dead, this brave and devoted missionary still speaks in the noble work which he accomplished in these islands; and the worshipping assemblies everywhere found in them are better monuments than those erected in Samoa and Rarotonga to his memory.

JOHN COLERIDGE PATTESON.

AMONG the islands in the South Pacific, near those visited and Christianized by the labors of Williams and his fellow-workers, is a group called Santa Cruz, lying north of the New Hebrides. Among all these islands, in years past, kidnapping vessels were accustomed to cruise, and decoy and steal as many of the natives as possible, and sell them into slavery. This aroused the passions of the natives, and, not knowing how to distinguish between white men who were friends and those who were foes, they generally revenged themselves on the first white visitors who arrived after a kidnapping had occurred. Thus the lamented Bishop Patteson, visiting one of these groups shortly after such an occurrence, was, though a devoted friend to the islanders, slain, as Williams had been, by the clubs of the natives, just as he was landing. Truly, the savages knew not what they did; for those clubs struck down one of their most devoted friends, and one in a position to do much towards securing their temporal and eternal welfare.

John Coleridge Patteson was born in London

in 1827. His father, Sir John Patteson, held a position on the English bench, and was highly esteemed as a lawyer. His mother was a niece of the poet Coleridge, whose name she gave to her son. In his boyhood the subject of our sketch is said to have been more than ordinarily quick in acquiring knowledge, reading well at five years of age; and from a very early period his mind was bent upon becoming a clergyman, a purpose which his mother took care to foster. When eight years of age he was sent to Ottery to school; and when he reached the age of eleven he was transferred to Eton, where he was noted as one of the best cricket-players in the school. While there he heard Dr. Selwyn, the newly-consecrated bishop of New Zealand, preach in New Windsor Chapel, and the sermon made a deep impression on his mind. Bishop Selwyn, being acquainted with the Patteson family, visited them before leaving England, and on leaving said to Lady Patteson, "You must give me Coley."

He entered Baliol College in his eighteenth year. After his graduation and ordination he accepted the position of curate at Affington; and while there he interested himself greatly in both the temporal and spiritual welfare of the poor of the parish. But while Patteson was thus engaged, Bishop Selwyn returned to England, and revived the young curate's aspirations for the work of a missionary. The consent of his father being obtained—his mother having before this been called home to her rest above—he sailed in March, 1855, for his life-work among the islands of the South Pacific.

Bishop Selwyn had established a college at Auckland, in New Zealand, and here Patteson began his first work—the work of assisting in the education of native missionaries. Bishop Selwyn's plan was to gather young boys from the islands around, teach them, and return them in his mission ship to their respective homes for the yearly vacation. These boys, even if not converted to Christ, yet, by their increased intelligence, and their reports of the work and worship at Auckland, were so many missionaries preparing the way for the acceptance of the gospel. Into this work Mr. Patteson entered with all the enthusiasm of his nature. Bishop Selwyn wrote to his father, some time after the arrival of the young man,

"Coley is, as you say, the right man in the right place, mentally and physically. The multiplicity of languages, which would try most men, is met by his peculiar gift. The heat of the climate suits his peculiar constitution; his mild and parental temper makes his black boys cling about him as their natural protector; his freedom from fastidiousness makes all parts of the work easy to him; for when you have to teach boys how to wash themselves and to wear clothes for the first time, the romance of missionary work disappears as completely as a great man's heroism before his *valet de chambre.*"

During the recess of the college studies, Mr. Patteson was accustomed to visit, in the missionary ship, other islands besides those from which they had students. In one of these voyages, the one undertaken in 1857, he visited sixty-six islands, and landed eighty-one times, being shot at by savage arrows only twice. He exchanged with the natives hatchets, gimlets, bottles, calico, etc., for cocoanuts, yams, and other products, thus securing the confidence of the natives, and opening the way either for obtaining boys for the college, or for sending a missionary to live and preach among the islanders.

In 1858 it was deemed desirable to establish another college, or, if that name is too dignified for these training schools, another school, at Lifu; and Mr. Patteson, with twelve boys from the Northwest Islands, speaking no fewer than six languages, was landed there. "He and four boys slept in one of the corner rooms, the other eight lads in another, and the Rarotongan teacher, Tatoo, and his wife, in a third." The building was not very costly, but, as a beginning, it suited the purpose. Mr. Patteson, however, soon removed the school to a more desirable location at St. Andrews, Kohimarama.

He describes his work here as follows: "I like quiet and rest, with no railroads and no daily posts, and, above all, no visitors, mere consumers of time, mere idlers and producers of idleness. So without any post, and nothing for a cart and wheels save a wheelbarrow, and no visitors and no shops, I get on very happily and contentedly. The life here is to me, I must confess, luxurious, because I have what I like: great punctuality, early hours, regular school work, regular reading, very simple living—the three daily meals in hall take about seventy minutes all put together; and so, little time is lost; and then the climate is delightful."

Thus the work in the schools went on, being in great measure preparatory to the greater work of procuring access for missionaries to the various islands. To such an extent was the latter enterprise engaged in that, to further it, it was proposed to consecrate Mr. Patteson a bishop, which was accordingly done February 24, 1861. Soon after he wrote to his father, "How I think of those islands, how I see those bright coral and sandy beaches, strips of burning sunshine fringing the masses of forest, rising into ridges of hills, covered with a dense mass of vegetation! Hundreds of people are crowding upon them, naked, armed, with wild, uncouth cries and gestures. I cannot talk to them but by signs. But they are my children now. May God enable me to do my duty to them."

The bishop now devoted himself even more fully than in the past to obtain scholars for his schools, as the best means of gaining the confidence of the natives. A few boys brought away and returned in a few months, clothed and improved somewhat in manners, were sure to gain the confidence of the whole island, and provide for a supply of boys beyond his demand. The difficulty was to obtain boys for the first time from an island. Mr. Whitehead, a mate of the missionary vessel, describes how it was done:

"There was much risk connected with these boating trips. The mode of procedure was for the schooner to stand in the smooth water on the lee side of the island to be visited. The bishop's whaleboat was then lowered, and manned by his own volunteer crew. . . . . But the difficulty, first of all, lay in landing. Even on the lee side of these islands there is often much surf, and in smooth water the coral reefs with which they are surrounded are dangerous neighbors for a boat's planking. And so it often happened that the boat remained outside the reef at a safe distance, while the bishop jumped overboard, and swam or waded ashore, as the case might be. And here, again, were new and still more terrible dangers, which that undaunted hero faced with extraordinary calmness and intrepidity. Perhaps, as was often the case, he desired to effect a landing at a new place, a village with which he had never previously held communication, of whose language he knew nothing. On the beach he would be met by a party of wild and fearful-looking savages, stark naked, and all armed with their cruel-looking clubs and spears, chattering, yelling, and brandishing their weapons like so many demons. .... I have seen him under such circumstances calmly advance up the beach into the very midst of such a party of ferocious beings. As he would advance they would close around him; his black coat would be lost sight of among their brown bodies; nothing could be seen but a brown mass and a vision of waving arms and ponderous clubs, while a chorus of yells would awaken the echoes of the shores. Then, after an interval, the brown mass might be seen steadily and slowly creeping towards the green skirting of scrub which backed the coral sands; one or two of the nude figures would dart out from the group and disappear, shouting, amid the tropical foliage. Additional forms could be observed emerging from behind bushes and trunks of trees, many of them women and children. Then, for a while, all would be quiet. Perhaps in half an hour the brown fellows would begin to assemble again on the beach; then more shouting. Then the bishop would come into view, leading by each hand a tiny brown boy. Then the brown mass, as before, gesticulating and shouting. Then the farewell; the bishop, turning, would make his last presents, shake hands with all who desired, and plunge into the surf with the two boys."

Thus boys were obtained from new islands by a process which required bravery superior to that which is needed to lead a forlorn hope on the battlefield. It demanded also devotion, tact, and skill such as can be found only in a heart consecrated to the Lord Jesus Christ.

The reception on landing was not always as in the case just described. A little later than this a visit was made to Santa Cruz, where three of the boat's crew were severely wounded with arrows, from which two of them died. It was a terrible grief to Bishop Patteson, and weighed upon his spirits for a long time.

His field of operation being chiefly among the

Melanesian Islands, he removed his school to Norfolk Island, some six hundred miles nearer than Auckland and St. Andrews, and also more desirable as respects climate. Here he enjoyed himself much in building up a Christian village. Occasionally he laid aside his robes of office, if he ever wore any, and cooked for himself some favorite dishes; and sometimes he baked bread, which he flattered himself was "uncommonly good."

But he drew near the end of his work. In April, 1871, he started on his last voyage among the islands of the New Hebrides group, and finally reached Santa Cruz, where, as we have already said, he died a martyr for the cause of Christ. Five wounds from a club ended the life consecrated to the renovation and salvation of these islanders. He was murdered by the same people who had, some years before, killed Fisher Young, his beloved friend, to whom, when dying, the bishop had said, "My dear boy, you will do more for their conversion by your death than ever we shall by our lives."

Thus a noble man and devoted missionary passed away. As a friend who knew him well said, in words quoted by Mr. Page in his "Noble Workers," the volume to which we are indebted for the facts in our sketch, he was "fearless as a man, tender as a woman, showing both the best sides of human nature, always drawing out the good in all about him by force of sympathy, and not only taking care that nothing should be done by others that he would not do himself, but doing himself what he did not like to ask of them, and thinking that they excelled him."

HEROINES.

ANNE ASKEW.

MORE than three hundred and thirty years ago, at Smithfield, London, a congregation was assembled to hear a sermon; in the midst of the assembly, and the object indeed of its meeting, was the subject of our sketch, a young lady of about twenty-five years. The sermon was for her special benefit; it was to prepare her for a fearful death, or, rather, for the judgment beyond death.

Anne Askew was the second daughter of Sir William Askew, of Lincolnshire, England. Her elder sister was betrothed to a gentleman who lived in the same county, and was reputed to be the possessor of large wealth. She died, however, before the marriage, and her father, unwilling to lose the benefit of the alliance, compelled Anne to marry the man who had pledged himself to her sister. The event became one means of leading Anne to seek consolation in the religion of Christ. As she had been blessed with a godly tutor, the divine source of comfort and strength in trial was known to her.

Though she conducted herself as a Christian

wife should, yet, her heart not having been given to her husband, loneliness and grief shadowed her steps, and led her to the truths of the Bible for comfort and direction. But her Bible reading soon alienated her mind from the doctrines and requirements of the Romish church, and trouble followed. Even her husband, the father of her two children, united with the priests in demanding that she should at once cease reading the Bible. This her conscience would not permit her to do; so her husband turned her out of doors, and with her two children she returned to her father's house. It is not known what reception she met there, but at any rate she was too near her husband's family to be allowed to remain in peace, and having some relatives in London, she removed thither, hoping to secure a divorce from her husband.

But she was not thus to escape the clutches of heresy-hunting Rome. Spies were set on her track, and finally she was summoned before the inquisitors in Sadler's Hall and questioned concerning her religious belief. Priests were sent to entrap her with questions, and at last Bishop Bonner undertook the case himself, drew up a paper asserting a belief in transubstantiation and in the regenerating influences of the sacraments of the church, and required her to subscribe to it. This she refused to do, unless justified by the expression, "I believe so much thereof as the Holy Scriptures do agree unto." Her answer excited the bishop's wrath, but for the time being she was released.

Some months after, however, she was re-arrested and confined in a cell in Newgate, from which she was taken and examined before the king's council, when she boldly declared her belief in the spiritual nature of the sacraments, and denied that the bread and wine actually changed into Christ's body and blood. Such a doctrine her judges would not tolerate, and she was condemned to be burned to death.

After her condemnation her judges determined to compel her to implicate others in holding the same doctrine. Accordingly, they put her upon the rack, and almost tore her limbs asunder; finally, when she swooned in the midst of her excruciating suffering, they desisted, and offered to pardon her if she recanted, which proposition she was enabled by the grace of God to spurn. Indeed, if she had recanted, her persecutors would probably have treated her as Cranmer was afterwards treated, and burned her as if she had not complied with their demand.

It was announced that she had recanted, whereupon a friend wrote to her asking her if the report was true. She replied as follows: "Oh, friend, most dearly beloved in God, I marvel not a little what should move you to judge in me so slender a faith as to fear death, which is the end of all misery. In the Lord I desire you not to believe of me such wickedness, for, I doubt it not, God will perform his work in me like as he hath begun. I understand the council is not a little displeased that it should be reported abroad that I was racked in the tower. They say now that what they did was but to force me: whereby I perceive they are ashamed of their uncomely doings, and fear much lest the king's majesty should have information thereof; therefore they would no man to noise it. Will God forgive them their cruelty? Your heart in Christ Jesus. Farewell, and pray."

She also wrote a beautiful prayer, in which occur the following expressions: "Now, Lord, I heartily desire of thee that thou wilt by thy most merciful goodness forgive them that violence which they do and have done to me. Open also thou their blind eyes, that they may hereafter do that thing in thy sight which is acceptable before thee."

But the end was near; the 16th of July, 1546, arrived. The lady, unable to stand after the torture which she had suffered, was borne in a chair to the stake, and bound to it with an iron chain.

Before the flame was kindled she was offered a pardon if she would recant; but she nobly replied, "I come not hither to deny my Lord and Master."

The lord mayor cried, "*Fiat justitia!*"—let justice be done—and Anne Askew passed to that rest which remaineth for the people of God.

Who can tell how many have been emboldened to confess Christ by the example of this youthful martyr? In the words appended to the narrative in the volume of "Noble English Women," to which we are chiefly indebted for our sketch,

"Flung to the heedless winds,
Or on the waters cast,
The martyr's ashes watched
Shall gathered be at last.
And from the scattered dust
Around us and abroad,
Shall spring a plenteous seed
Of witnesses for God."

LADY MARGARET DOUGLAS.

THIS noble lady was a daughter of the Earl of Morton, and was born in Scotland in 1610, a few years after the death of Queen Elizabeth. The queen's successor, James the First of England and Sixth of Scotland, soon exerted his influence against the Presbyterian Church, an opposition continued by his successors, to the great sorrow and suffering of the subject of our sketch. At an early age she was married to Lord Lorne, who afterwards became Marquis of Argyll. He was distinguished for his piety and for his adherence to the cause of Presbyterianism, and in his wife he found a noble helpmeet. Even in that age of suffering for Christ's cause and covenant they were noted for their deep piety. It is said that they not only observed family worship morning and evening, but that together they spent portions of the day in more private devotions. But her piety could not exempt her from the law "that we must through much tribulation enter into the kingdom of God."

Her first great grief was caused by the unprincipled conduct of Charles II. His father,

Charles I., had subverted the Presbyterian constitution of the Church of Scotland, legally established in 1592, by forcing upon it, in 1636, his primate Laud's Book of Canons and Liturgy, virtually making the Scottish church prelatic, and binding its ministry to doctrines which they regarded as subversive of the Word of God and of civil and religious liberty.

The tyranny and perfidy of Charles brought him to the block, January 30, 1649. His son, having arrived in Scotland, was crowned king at Scone, January 1, 1651, the Marquis of Argyll placing the crown on his head. In order to attract the support of Presbyterians, the young king engaged himself to the marquis' daughter, but, doubtless, with no thought of carrying out his agreement. After his engagement his conduct was such that the marquis felt compelled to reprove him in private; whereupon he shed tears, and prayed that God would enable him to walk more circumspectly in the future. When the marchioness was informed of Charles' behavior she was greatly troubled; she felt that his tears were hypocritical, and that he never would forgive her husband for reproving him; and the sequel showed that she read his character aright. In the meantime, her daughter was so mortified by the conduct of Charles that she became insane, and thus was a continued living trial to her mother.

But still greater trials awaited the Marchioness of Argyll. A change took place in the sentiments of the English people. Charles, who had escaped to the Continent, was recalled, and sailed from the Hague for London, arriving there in May, 1660. After being securely seated on the throne he remembered the presumption of Argyll in reproving him for his wickedness, and ordered his trial for high treason. This was the second severe affliction that his wife was called to endure; but, like Job, she held fast her trust in God, and "in seasons of her deepest distress she betook herself to the throne of grace," where she obtained strength to sustain her, and also to enable her to comfort those around her. She felt sure, as soon as her husband was committed to prison, that Charles would be satisfied with nothing less than his life. She therefore arranged a plan for her husband's escape from prison, which would doubtless have been successful; but when the time for its execution came, he said, "I will not flee from the cause I have so publicly owned." He preferred to die, rather than seem to betray the cause of truth and righteousness. Accordingly, he was sentenced to death by the venal court which tried him. One of the principal charges against him was his entering into "the solemn league and covenant" of Scotland with England, in 1643, which for a time won Scottish support for the Parliamentary cause against Charles I. We can easily imagine the distress of the marchioness on hearing of the sentence pronounced against her husband. She instantly sought his prison to sympathize with him, and was herself encouraged by his declaration, "They may shut me in where they please, but they cannot shut out God from me." She next exerted all her energy to obtain a reprieve, but without avail; her husband was executed May 25, 1661, and his head was fixed on the west end of the Tolbooth prison at Edinburgh. As the day of execution drew near, his wife spent a large portion of her time in prayer; and God heard her cry, and gave wonderful serenity to the mind of her husband, so that he could address his fellow-citizens from the scaffold with composure.

In 1681 the marchioness' cup of affliction was again filled by the unjust trial for treason, and the condemnation of her eldest son, who, however, for a time escaped from the hands of his enemies by flight to Holland. But a few years after his mother's death, his love for Protestantism led him to engage in the Duke of Monmouth's rising against James II., and, being taken prisoner, he was put to death as a traitor, June 30, 1685.

Amid all the sorrows of the marchioness the grace of God sustained her; and for the seventeen years during which she survived her husband she devoted herself chiefly to relieving the necessities of the poor about her residence near Roseneath, a beautiful village on the Clyde. Her pastor testified concerning her, after her death, that "she had endured a sore, a tedious and constant fight of afflictions, yet was she enabled to bear through with that faith, patience, submission, and Christian magnanimity that were very visible, commendable, and exemplary; and such diligence and assiduity in following the duties of praying, reading, hearing, praise, and all the acts of worship; a constant waiting upon all ordinances and duties, public and private; and even upon the weekly catechising, at which she delighted to be present, and by which she confessed that she profited much."

On March 13, 1678, she was taken home to her Father's house. She had lived nearly sixty-eight years, amid joys and sorrows, experiencing more than ordinary vicissitudes in her life, and passing through a period of cruel persecution to the church, a period when many of its noblest ministers, such as Guthrie, McKail, and Cargill, were put to death because they maintained the supremacy of the Lord Jesus Christ as King and Head of his church, and would not cease preaching his gospel, though they had to do it as described by the Scottish poet James Grahame, in his admirable poem on the Sabbath:

> "No more
> The assembled people dared, in face of day,
> To worship God; or even at the dead
> Of night, save when the wintry storms were fierce,
> And thunder-peals compelled the men of blood
> To couch within their dens."

It was also in this period, however, that God visited his people in the revival at Shotts, and in the stirring of religious fervor leading to the adoption and subscription of the national "covenant," when sixty thousand people assembled, on February 28, 1638, in the Greyfriars' church and churchyard at Edinburgh, and put their names to the paper which engaged them at all hazards to support their faith and principles to the end. All such scenes had special interest for the Marchioness of Argyll, and as a devoted Christian woman her name deserves a record in the history of the church.

MRS. ISABELLA GRAHAM.

NEAR Paisley, in the woods of Eldersley—a name famous in Scotland as the home of the patriot Sir William Wallace—between the years 1750 and 1752, a little girl, under ten years of age, might frequently have been seen passing thoughtfully from and to her home. It was Isabella Marshall, afterwards the well-known philanthropist, Mrs. Graham, going to or returning from the sacred spot where she first dedicated herself to God, and where she delighted, as Rutherford would say, "to keep tryst" with Him, and pour into his ear all her childish troubles. Her father had sold his paternal estate near Hamilton, where Isabella was born in July, 1742, and removed to this pleasant home. The church with which he had there connected himself had then for its pastor Dr. Witherspoon, afterwards president of Princeton College, and one of the boldest advocates of American independence. It was through his influence, years afterwards, that the valuable services of Mrs. Graham were secured to the city of New York.

Her godly grandfather, who was one of the

MRS. ISABELLA GRAHAM. 277

associates of Ebenezer and Ralph Erskine when they seceded from the Established Church of Scotland in 1733 and 1737, bequeathed to her one hundred pounds, and she requested that it might be used in securing her an education. Thus God provided the means for her necessary training for her noble work. In her twenty-third year she was married to Dr. John Graham, then a practising physician in Paisley, but afterwards appointed surgeon to the Royal American regiment stationed at Montreal. Here Dr. and Mrs. Graham joined the regiment, which was soon, however, removed to Fort Niagara, on Lake Ontario, where they remained four years. But, being destitute of the public ordinances of religion and of the opportunity of engaging in work for Christ and his cause, Mrs. Graham confessed that she made no progress in the divine life.

The regiment was next ordered to the island of Antigua, to which place Dr. and Mrs. Graham, with their little family, consisting of three infant daughters and two Indian nurse girls, began their journey. Dr. Graham hoped, however, to sell his commission in New York, purchase land on the Mohawk River, and remain in the northern colonies. But he failed in this project, and proceeded to his destination with his family. In 1774, while at Antigua, he was seized with an illness which terminated in his death. The fact that he was prepared for this event, that his trust was in the only Saviour, soothed somewhat the sorrow of the bereaved and lonely widow. She was indeed in a pitiable condition, left with three daughters, the oldest not over five years, with little property, and at a distance from home and friends. But she was roused from her sorrow to plan for her children, and such was her trust in God that she did not covet "an independent fortune." It was enough for her that she could daily tell her Heavenly Father of her wants, and feel sure he would supply them.

After the birth of a son, a few months after her husband's death, Mrs. Graham, with her four little ones and one of the Indian girls, embarked for Belfast, Ireland, intending to proceed thence to Scotland. The vessel in which she sailed from Ireland was wrecked on the coast of Ayr, and the passengers and crew narrowly escaped with their lives. Mrs. Graham was the only one found free from fear during this time of peril. Peacefully she gathered her children around her, saying, "Now we shall all, in a few minutes, be with father in a better world."

But her work was not yet done. The storm subsided and they were saved, and in a few days she reached her father's house. This was not the large mansion of Eldersley, but a little thatched cottage of three apartments. Her father had been induced to become security for some of his friends, and was now reduced to poverty. Her mother had previously died, and her father was now added to her children as one of her dependents. But God could help them all, and he did.

Mrs. Graham soon removed to Paisley, where she opened a school and taught for a time. She had to make her breakfast and supper of porridge, and dinner of potatoes and salt. Yet she labored on until her Heavenly Father saw that she was prepared for her great work among the poor of New York, and then he opened the way for her to begin it. But those early years of her widowhood held many an anxious and sorrowful day, and it is said that the tears which she shed injured her eyes, and made it necessary for her to use spectacles at a very early age.

She was persuaded by her friends to move to Edinburgh in 1780, to open a school for the education of young ladies. There she was very successful, and formed lasting friendships with such noble women as Viscountess Glenorchy, a sketch of whom is included in the present work. There Mrs. Graham's children received the greater part of their education, and there her father died, surrounded with all the comforts of a happy home.

There she founded "the Penny Society," for the aid of the poor when sick, which has now become an important institution. To show the position of influence to which she attained in the capital of her native land, it may be mentioned that Lady Glenorchy arranged that whenever she should be laid on her dying-bed, Mrs. Graham must be sent for, no matter where she might be. She, accordingly, was present to close the eyes of her friend, and she was remembered by her in her will.

Dr. Witherspoon, the pastor of her girlhood, persuading Mrs. Graham that New York city would be a better field for her energies, she removed, in 1789, to New York, where for years she exerted a most powerful and beneficial influence. In her school, which at once became popular, she inculcated "the principles of religion as the only solid foundation for morality and virtue." As she had the faculty of winning the affection of her pupils, and impressing her principles upon their hearts, and as those pupils were from the most influential families of the city, she had the opportunity of doing a great work for our country.

But she was not content with her school work, noble as it was. She sought other fields of usefulness. In 1797 she instituted "the Society for the Relief of Poor Widows with Small Children."

She knew from her own experience the need of aid in such circumstances. Then, with Mrs. Hoffman and others, she established the "Orphan Asylum Society;" then "the Magdalene Society;" then "the Society for the Promotion of Industry Among the Poor." She became also herself a tract and Bible distributer. Before the institution of the Bible and Tract Societies, she published tracts, purchased Bibles, and distributed them in her daily visits in the homes of the poor. She also commenced several Sabbath-schools, probably the first in America, though they were intended for adults. Thus her head, heart, and hands were busy in the work of the Lord.

Mrs. Graham's three daughters developed into noble women, and were married to leading citizens in New York; and no doubt her descendants are still prominent in the work of the Lord in our land. Her son, from the mistaken idea then prevalent that women are not capable of training boys, was put under other influences, and did not live to honor the name of either his father or his mother; and yet, judging from the last letter received from him by his loving mother, he probably died trusting in the Saviour "whose blood cleanseth from all sin."

During Mrs. Graham's absence from the city, her daughter, Mrs. Bethune, was surprised at the frequent inquiries made for her by people whom she did not know; at length she asked some of the inquirers what they knew about Mrs. Graham, and received the answer, "She used to visit our neighborhood, and relieve and comfort the poor; and we used to watch and see her pass, and bless her for her kindness; and we were afraid she was sick, as we had not seen her for so long." Verily, the poor arose and called her blessed.

Like the apostle Paul, she could rejoice even in her tribulations. In a letter to a friend she wrote, "When matters have been at the worst with me as to this world, my triumphs in my God have been highest, and prospects for eternity brightest."

But the years passed, and on July 19, 1814, the diligent hand and the loving heart were laid upon a bed of sickness which was to prove a bed of death. A dear friend was sent for, who had agreed with Mrs. Graham that the survivor should attend the dying-bed of the other. When Mrs. Chrystie entered the room she was greeted with the exclamation, "I am going to get the start of you. I am called home before you. It will be your office to fill our engagement."

To her children Mrs. Graham said, "I have no more doubt of going to my Saviour than if I were already in his arms. My guilt is all transferred. He has cancelled all I owed; yet I could weep for sins against so good a God."

For some days she lingered, conversing with her friends and enjoying their prayers and readings, especially some of the hymns which exalt the grace found in the Lord Jesus Christ; and on the morning of July 27, 1814, with a smile, and the word "peace," she passed into the presence of her Saviour.

Her departure was alluded to in the sermons of many of the leading ministers of the city. Her own pastor, Dr. Mason, delivered a memorial discourse which was published; and it is believed that great good has been effected through its circulation, as well as through the little volume by Mrs. Graham's daughter, Mrs. Bethune, to which latter we are chiefly indebted for the facts of our sketch. How much may be accomplished by a life consecrated to the cause of God and humanity! and how true it is that "the memory of the just is blessed!"

ELIZABETH FRY.

Not quite a hundred years ago, a young lady at Earlham Hall, near Norwich, England, wrote in her diary, "I am like a ship at sea without a pilot." She was mistaken; there was a Pilot very near her, One who loved her, One who was preparing her for a great work in the world, though she knew it not.

Many a wanderer in this sin-stricken world feels as if he were helpless, useless, and alone, while all the time the Saviour is whispering in his ear, "Thou art a chosen vessel unto me to bear my name before those who know me not." Thus it was with Elizabeth Gurney; but she did not know the voice that called, and did not wish to hear it, until some years afterwards, when she learned the meaning of the expression, "My sheep hear my voice, and I know them, and they follow me."

She was born near Norwich, in May, 1780. Her father and mother belonged to the denomination called "Friends," though they did not adhere strictly to all their peculiar customs. Her father was a man of wealth, and was engaged in the business of banking. Her mother was a great-granddaughter of Robert Barclay, a companion of George Fox, the founder of the Society of Friends. To her, doubtless, we are indebted, next to the grace of God, for Elizabeth's noble character.

Of that mother she wrote, years afterwards, "I loved my mother dearly. I used to be in constant fear that she would die. Often in my little bed at night this would make me weep. I would go softly and watch her breathing, to convince myself that she was alive. We had a dear, good, wise mother, who wished nothing so much as that we might know the love and mercy of God in Christ, and the blessedness of his service."

That dear mother was soon taken from her, though not before her image was deeply impressed upon Elizabeth's heart; but when the brothers and sisters at Earlham Hall no longer witnessed the godly example of their devoted mother, the Bible was not read as frequently or as seriously as in the days gone by.

As Elizabeth grew older she began to realize the truth of the prophet's declaration, "The heart is deceitful above all things, and desperately wicked;" but how to get a new heart she did not know.

At length William Savery, a Friend from America, came to preach in the meeting-house at

Norwich. He told of a Saviour who wishes to be received into the heart, a Saviour who can cleanse it from sin, as well as save from sin's penalty. Listening to him, Elizabeth was enabled at least to desire that Saviour to come in and dwell with her; and great was her joy for many weeks in the experience of what she thought was the Saviour's love. As she was now a young lady, it was thought proper, at about this time, that she should go to London and be initiated into the ways of the fashionable world. But in those ways she found no real enjoyment, though fascinated with them for a time; deep down in her heart she was desiring something better. So she returned, and commenced a school for the poor in the neighborhood of her home, also visiting the sick, and supplying their wants. It was a preparation for the greater work she was soon to undertake in London. In a short time she not only desired the Saviour, but rejoiced in him as hers; and after this she became the joy of the home circle, as well as of the whole neighborhood.

But the poor of Norwich and the school-children whom she had gathered were soon to be deprived of her care. It was whispered that Elizabeth Gurney was about to leave Earlham Hall and live in London, and ere long Joseph Fry, a wealthy banker, came and carried her away, and

Elizabeth Gurney became Mrs. Fry, the name by which she is best known. Soon the poor found her in her new home; soon she found the poor in the lanes and alleys, and finally in the asylums and prisons; and no doubt many said of her, "The blessing of him that was ready to perish came upon" her, and she "caused the widow's heart to sing for joy."

In the year 1813 some members of the Society of Friends went to Newgate to visit certain persons there under sentence of death, and found the prison in a horrible condition. "There were in the prison four hundred women, old and young, with many little children, all crowded into four rooms. They were clothed in rags, with not a comfort apparently—no bedding, not even a pillow, only boards raised from the floor. There they lived day and night, ate, cooked, washed, and slept, with no employment, nothing to read, spending the time in swearing and fighting, or clambering at the iron bars, begging from visitors, and spending the money for liquor at a shop kept in the prison for their use."

Mrs. Fry was appealed to, and soon visited this sad scene, venturing alone to enter the rooms and counsel the lost inmates. After a while she proposed to teach them to read and write and work, so that when their terms of imprisonment should expire they might become respectable servants, at least. But at that period she had few sympathizers. Her best friends would say to her, "Dear Mrs. Fry, what a wild plan you have got in your head! Do you suppose that women who have broken the laws of the land will obey you? If you give them work, they will steal it or tear it up. No, indeed, there is not the least hope for such degraded mortals." But they did not understand the power of love as Mrs. Fry did. She persevered, and wonderful was her success. The poor, depraved women of the prisons could be reached by the gospel of love, and the effect of Mrs. Fry's visitations began to be the talk not only of London, but of the United Kingdom.

One day, while she was reading the Scriptures aloud in prison, according to her custom, Sir William Curtis, lord mayor of London, four aldermen, and the sheriffs, stepped into the room. Mrs. Fry stopped reading for a moment, but was requested to go on as usual. After the reading the prisoners began their work, sewing or knitting, as the case might be. Their neat appearance, obedient manners, and happy faces, so different from what these gentlemen had been accustomed to see, perfectly astonished them. The old beer-shop had been quite broken up by this time, and a respectable notion and grocery store had taken its place.

The reading of the Word of God was greatly blessed to the prisoners, and many were converted to God by it. In the meantime Mrs. Fry was receiving letters not only from different places in Great Britain, but even from Russia and India, inquiring concerning the mode of her work, that it might be put in practice in other prisons. Princes from the Continent visited her during the hours devoted to her work in prison, to learn the secret of her wonderful success; and no doubt great reforms in the treatment of prisoners all over the world resulted. When King Kamehameha, of the Sandwich Islands, wanted to prevent intoxicating drinks from being exported to his dominions, he wrote to Mrs. Fry to secure his purpose. When, after a few years, she visited various countries on the Continent, kings and nobles vied with each other in the effort to do her honor; and when the king of Prussia visited England he called to see Mrs. Fry at her own home, and dined with her and her family, being introduced to her seven daughters and daughters-in-law, her seven sons, and her twenty-five grandchildren. And here it is proper to say that in accomplishing the public work to which she devoted herself she did not neglect the training of her own children.

Nor was what we have mentioned all her work. She took an interest in the coast-guard service, and finally succeeded in introducing libraries into all the stations, 623 in all, at a cost of $7,500. Then she turned her attention to putting good reading matter on board the vessels which sailed from Falmouth harbor. Mrs. Fry was also far in advance of the majority of professed Christians in her ideas of religious toleration, and she was successful in aiding persecuted evangelical denominations in Germany and Denmark.

The actual work which she herself accomplished was, however, scarcely so valuable as the example that she gave to the world of the true mode of helping the poor and depraved classes of the community. That example is now largely followed wherever Christianity prevails; and it will continue to bear fruit until time shall be no longer. Mrs. Fry's life shows what noble deeds a woman may accomplish when her heart is filled with a love for Christ and her spirit imbued with the principles of the gospel.

But time hastened on, Mrs. Fry reached her sixty-sixth year, and the messenger came, October 12, 1845, to take her home, "to see the King in his beauty," and to experience the meaning of the text, "Blessed are the dead which die in the Lord."

MARY LUNDIE DUNCAN.

Mrs. Sigourney thus wrote concerning the subject of our present sketch:

> "Sweet bird of Scotia's tuneful clime,
>   So beautiful and dear,
> Whose music gushed as genius taught,
> With heaven's own quenchless spirit fraught,
>   I list thy strain to hear.
>
> . . . .
>
> "Meek Christian, it is well with thee,
>   That where thy heart so long
> Was garnered up, thy home should be—
> Thy path with him who made thee free—
>   Thy lay an angel's song."

And well did she deserve this eulogy, as we shall see as we follow her in her short but devoted life. She was born in the year 1814, in the Manse of Kelso, her father, Rev. Robert Lundie, being pastor of the parish. She early exhibited unusual natural ability, and before she was five years old she could read with understanding. Many incidents of her childish days show wonderful thoughtfulness. Once, for example, when she was reading in the Bible, with her brother, about Elymas the sorcerer being struck blind, her brother exclaimed, "I would have stricken him dumb for speaking against the gospel." She replied, "Oh no, Corrie; blinding him was best, for he might repent, and then he could speak for the gospel."

From her own account, given in her thirteenth year, when she was permitted publicly to confess her Saviour at the communion table, the Holy Spirit convinced her of her need of the Saviour as early as her seventh year, and from that time prayer, praise, and doing her Master's will gave her delight.

She very early showed a talent for writing poetry. The following is a specimen written in or before her twelfth year:

> "How sweet are those delightful dreams
>   That charm in youth's first days of bloom!
> And sweet those radiant sunshine gleams
>   That wander through surrounding gloom.
>
> "And bright are fancy's fairy bowers,
>   And sweet the flowers that round she flings,
> When, in gay youth's romantic hours,
>   She shows all fair and lovely things.
>
> "But, ah! there is a land above,
>   Whose pleasures never fade away;
> A holy land of bliss and love,
>   Where night is lost in endless day.
>
> "And in the blaze of that blest day,
>   All earthly bowers we deemed so bright
> Must fade, as when the sun's first ray
>   Dispels the darkness of the night."

After spending some years in London in a boarding-school, where she set a good example of meekness, piety, and adherence to principle, she returned, in her seventeenth year, to Kelso, and began work in the Sabbath-school as a teacher. This work was to her a delight, as is evident from the following extract from a letter to a friend: "There is far more peace and satisfaction in living to be useful than in anything else, if the action spring from that animating motive, love to Him who so much loves us." Very soon after this was written she greatly needed the sustaining power of divine love, for her father was suddenly called to his heavenly home, in April, 1832. She was deeply wounded by the sudden blow, but she knew where healing could be found, not being a stranger to the great Physician, who can bind up broken hearts, as well as save souls.

Some time after this she became engaged to Mr. Duncan, a licentiate of the Established Church of Scotland, and son of a special friend of her father. Anxiously he looked, waited, and prayed for an appointment to a field of labor, that the relation of husband and wife might be consummated. At length he was presented to the parish of Urr by the patron, but it was just at the time when many in the Established Church were beginning to protest against patronage; and though the congregation at Urr had no special objection to Mr. Duncan, they nevertheless rejected him, and were sustained by the church courts.

Thus Miss Lundie's fond hopes, when almost realized, were dashed to the ground. Her disappointment, however, was the means of calling forth some letters which, we think, cannot be read without leaving on the heart of the reader a desire for greater consecration to God.

But by-and-by the dark cloud was lifted. A call from the people of Cleish, and the presentation from its patron, were given to Mr. Duncan, and the way was thus opened for the union of these two loving hearts. In 1836 they were married, and went to their new home and work. Soon after Mrs. Duncan wrote in her diary, "Our income amply supplies our present wants, and when the thought of the future comes over me, I turn it into a prayer for increase of faith, for what have the future and I to do with each other? How numerous are our blessings! His people love him, the surrounding families here have received me kindly, we have lovely scenery around, and are engaged in the most honorable work that can employ mortal man. Shall we not raise here our Ebenezer, and bless the Lord who hath done so great things for us?"

Heartily she engaged in the work of the parish with her husband, as may be seen from the following extract from a letter to her friend E——:
"I have just begun to distribute tracts, and hope these little silent visitors may prove messengers of peace to some around us. I have only undertaken fifteen houses, as my time will hardly admit of more. I like the work very much, as it enables me to speak of eternal things, making an opening for me. There are in the parish a few drops of blessing, but, oh, where is the refreshing shower that should make our wilderness blossom as the rose?"

Domestic work now began to claim more attention from Mrs. Duncan. It pleased her Heavenly Father to send her a little daughter, and then a son, to train for Him; and nobly did she fulfil her task. Among other things, she addressed to them hymns which, doubtless, in after years were regarded with affectionate reverence. We give a few verses selected from several:

> "Jesus, Saviour, pity me;
> Hear me when I cry to thee!
> I've a very naughty heart,
> Full of sin in every part;
> I can never make it good;
> Wilt thou wash me in thy blood?
> Jesus, Saviour, pity me;
> Hear me when I cry to thee!"

> "Jesus, tender Shepherd, hear me;
> Bless thy little lamb to-night;
> Through the darkness be thou near me,
> Watch my sleep till morning light."

> "What sound is this that gently falls
> Upon the quiet air?
> It is the Sabbath bell that calls
> Men to the house of prayer;
> For there God promises to meet
> All those who worship at his feet."

Her last poetic production was addressed to her brother George, some nine months before her death, on his leaving to seek restoration to health in Australia. It ends as follows:

> "But go, heaven's blessing on thy path attending,
> Where nature's glories shine on frozen hearts;
> And as the sun, the veil of darkness rending,
> His morning splendor o'er creation darts,
> May gospel beams diffuse resplendent day,
> To guide the hapless flock that darkling stray.

> "How beautiful on earth's dark hills appearing,
> Day's harbinger, the messenger of peace!
> How sweet his earnest voice the wanderer cheering,
> That tells of morn arising, ne'er to cease.
> Bear thou those tidings o'er the heaving main,
> And turned to songs shall be our parting pain."

She had such enjoyment in her work, her husband, and her children, that she felt that her happiness was too great to be long continued in this sin-stricken world, where we all need to be reminded that this is not our rest. And her premonition was soon verified. The 5th of January, 1840, was drawing nearer and nearer—the day that was to mark the limit of earth's joys and sorrows to her. She was only twenty-five years old, but her work was done, the crown was ready for her brow, the shining messengers were commissioned to take her home. She was laid to rest in "God's acre," in the parish churchyard of Cleish, until the resurrection of the just. She left behind her an example, telling how much may be done by the quiet, every-day life of a consecrated Christian woman. Her life was not like the sudden flash of a meteor over the sky, but rather like the rays of the morning sun, shining brighter and brighter until its meridian splendor is attained. We cannot point to any wonderful work accomplished by her at any particular time, but we have no doubt that many were born into the kingdom of heaven through her instrumentality; and though dead, she yet speaks in the memoir of her life compiled by her loving mother.

HANNAH MORE.

In a small thatched cottage in the parish of Stapleton, a few miles from Bristol, England, were passed the early years of one who, by her pen, was to exert a powerful influence upon society at home and abroad, an influence extending to all classes, from the highest to the lowliest.

Hannah More was born at Stapleton, February 2, 1745, being the fourth of a family of five daughters. Her father, having lost his fortune in a lawsuit, was the master of the village school, and there his daughters received the first rudiments of their education. Hannah showed from her earliest years wonderful precocity, and her father, encouraged by it, began to teach her his favorite Latin. Amazed at her rapid progress, he soon ceased, however, lest she should become a pedant; but through the persuasion of her mother the study was again permitted.

The income of a village school was not sufficient to provide for five young ladies in idleness, and the three elder daughters determined to follow their father's profession in Bristol. A private school was opened by them, in which they were

very successful, and after a while little Hannah became a pupil, and afterwards a teacher. Her superior abilities, and especially her conversational power, attracted attention and secured her many friends. At the age of seventeen her first volume, a pastoral drama, designed for recitation in schools, was issued, under the title of "The Search After Happiness."

The sisters were successful beyond expectation in their school, and after a while Sarah and Hannah determined to visit London and become acquainted with the noted men and women there. The famous "Blue Stocking Club" was then in its glory, and included among its members Mrs. Montagu, Mrs. Chapone, Elizabeth Carter, and others; to these Hannah More was introduced, and among them she made many life-long friends. She was also kindly received by Sir Joshua Reynolds, Dr. Johnson, David Garrick, and his wife. Mr. and Mrs. Garrick especially pleased her, and when visiting London she often made her home at their house. Probably through the friendship of Garrick she was led to write dramas for the stage; several of these were very successful, and at the time she thought she was doing something to promote good morals. But soon she had occasion to change her mind, and she afterwards wrote, "I was led to entertain what I must now think a delusive hope, that the stage, under certain regulations, might be converted into a school of virtue; that though a bad play would always be a bad play, yet the representation of a good one might become not only harmless, but useful. . . . . The fruits of the Spirit and the fruits of the stage, if the parallel were followed up, would exhibit as pointed a contrast as human imagination could conceive."

Both the church and the world have changed somewhat in manners since that period. The following is a description of an assemblage at the house of a bishop of the Church of England: "Conceive to yourself one hundred and fifty or two hundred people met together, dressed in the extremity of fashion, painted as red as bacchanals, poisoning the air with perfumes, treading on each other's gowns, making the crowd they blame, not one in ten able to get a chair, protesting they are engaged to ten other places, and lamenting the fatigue they are not obliged to endure; ten or a dozen card-tables crammed with dowagers of quality, grave ecclesiastics, and yellow admirals; and you have an idea of an assembly." Nor were these assemblages wholly confined to week-days. But Hannah More absolutely refused ever to attend one on Sunday.

She was a great admirer of Dr. Johnson, whom

she often met, and was cordially received by the gruff old moralist. She describes his last days as follows: "How solemn are the closing scenes of this dying man. He is styled the Moralist. Justice, truth, virtue were the pillars of his character; at all times and in all places he was loyal to his convictions of duty and reverent to God. In the wide grasp of his clear, calm, comprehensive mind he everywhere discerned a moral government and recognized a righteous Governor; his conscience, unswerved by passion or self-indulgence, spoke solemnly and was heard; the fear of God was upon him; but now, as the curtains of death close around his brave heart and unclouded intellect, he lies helpless, wrestling for hope, panting for peace, raising his eyes with a fearful looking-for of judgment. . . . . The man whose intellectual powers had awed all around him was now trembling, hopeless, unless external help is obtained. But that help was obtained, and he could declare that, though there was no salvation but in the Lamb of God, there was salvation there."

The success of Miss More's writings furnished her with a comfortable income, and she purchased a thatched cottage, with a flower-garden, at Cowslip Green, a few miles from Bristol. Here, with Patty, her younger sister, she took up her residence, and began her attack on the ungodly and immoral usages and customs of the times. Her first volume from this new home was entitled, "Thoughts on the Importance of the Manners of the Great to General Society." It appeared anonymously, in 1788, and was attributed to the Bishop of London, William Wilberforce, and others. The book was a success, seven editions being sold in a few months. Two years afterwards the author's "Estimate of the Religion of the Fashionable World" appeared, in which she attacked the too common custom of putting formal observances of Christian duty for heart-piety; the giving of a few dollars to a worthy cause, in the place of confession of sin and humble devotion to the divine Redeemer. The book was highly commended, and is worth reading still.

The writer was too noble a worker to remain hidden, and Wilberforce sought her out to engage her influence for the work to which he was at this time especially devoted—the abolition of the slave trade and the emancipation of the slaves in the West India Islands. He found her a willing and efficient helper, for she had a heart and a hand for every good work.

Mr. Wilberforce visited her in her home at Cowslip Green, and in exploring the romantic cliffs of Cheddar in the neighborhood, he found that in that village, so near the city of Bristol, distressing poverty and heathenish ignorance and immorality abounded. With a sad heart he returned to the cottage of his hostess, and on consultation with her, it was determined to do something to alleviate the condition of the villagers, Mr. Wilberforce becoming responsible for the expense of conducting the enterprise. This was the beginning of that system of mission-schools which the sisters inaugurated, and which accomplished so much for the poor of the parishes in the neighborhood of their dwellings. The need of such schools can easily be seen from the fact that in a neighboring parish the curate was frequently intoxicated, and sometimes unable to preach on account of black eyes received in alehouse fights. Happily, such clergymen would not now be tolerated in any parish in England.

Such, however, was the opposition of the people to anything like evangelical religion, that it required tact equal to that now necessary in our foreign missionaries to accomplish the requisite work. But Hannah More was equal to the task; a noble work was done in several adjoining parishes, and an example was set which doubtless has been followed by philanthropists in other places.

The period had now arrived when the French Revolution filled the prisons of France, deluged the streets of Paris with blood, and produced discontent among the workingmen in the neighboring kingdoms, including England.

Paley was appealed to, to write a book to quiet the excitement, and he published "Reasons for Contentment," for which he was made a prebend of St. Paul's; but the work was better suited to the minds of the educated class than to the masses of the people. Something simple, but full of wit and good common sense, was needed; and Hannah More, under the assumed name of "Will Chip," supplied it. In a few weeks after publication, her "Village Politics" found its way to palace, hall, and cottage, and the king, lords, bishops, and commons were loud in its praise. The Bishop of London said of it, "I look upon Mr. Chip as one of the finest writers of the age; this work alone will immortalize him, and, what is better still, I trust it will immortalize the constitution."

Soon after this Mrs. More commenced the publication of the "Cheap Repository," a monthly magazine, in which appeared her celebrated tract, "The Shepherd of Salisbury Plains," and also "Black Giles the Poacher," "Sorrowful Sam," and such ballads as "The Two Weavers," which illustrate the Christian tact by which she could reach the masses, and inspire them with contentment in the present and hopefulness for the future.

Mrs. More's pen was now kept busy, and whatever she produced was at once widely read, so that perhaps she was the most influential person in the kingdom as far as forming the character of the people was concerned. Her popularity also secured her funds with which she could prosecute her charitable work, and make herself and her sisters comfortable; and, at the same time, it enabled her to entertain the numerous friends who came to see her. But for this latter purpose her little cottage was now too small. She accordingly built a new mansion, and called it "Barley Wood;" it was a short distance from the old home, but in a far more desirable situation, overlooking the Wrington valley and the Atlantic ocean, with islands in the distance. To this beautiful home all the sisters removed, closing the school and house in Bristol, in 1801. Here Mrs. More still plied her pen, devoted to seeking the temporal and eternal welfare of her readers, and produced such works as "Cœlebs in Search of a Wife," "Practical Piety," "Christian Morals," etc. Here also she entertained her friends, among whom were Dr. Porteus, Bishop of London, John Newton, William Wilberforce, and noted visitors from our own and other lands.

After nearly twelve years in this loved home, death called Mary, the oldest sister, away. Elizabeth was next removed, and then Sally, Hannah and her younger sister Patty being left to manage their home and look after the schools, where they continued to do a great work for Christ and humanity. Other friends were also called away, and among them Mrs. Garrick, in her hundredth year. Finally, in 1819, the much-loved and sprightly Patty was taken away, after a very brief but painful illness, and Hannah was left to finish her journey alone. But she did not cease her work. She scattered her wealth with a liberal hand, and by an extensive correspondence did much to foster many a good cause.

After enjoying the beauties of "Barley Wood" for twenty-seven years, Mrs. More was persuaded to take a smaller house in Clifton, where she still entertained her friends and gave her voice and pen to the proclamation of the Lord Jesus Christ as the sinner's Saviour, and of Christianity as the antidote to the world's woe. At last, on September 7th, 1833, in the eighty-ninth year of her age, she fell asleep in Jesus, and her body was consigned to its rest in the family vault at Wrington.

MARY SOMERVILLE.

Less than a hundred years ago, a little girl in Burntisland, Scotland, discovered an old book filled with such characters as $x+y=a$, $12x+7y=10a$. She was very much astonished at the curious book, and many were her inquiries until she found out what was the use of it. By-and-by she was introduced to Euclid, a very unusual study at that time for a woman. But she persevered in her application to mathematics, until Mary Somerville was known as one of the first mathematicians of her day.

She was born at Burntisland, on the Frith of Forth, opposite Edinburgh. Her father was a naval officer, who distinguished himself in several engagements, and was afterwards known as Admiral Sir William Fairfax. He was necessarily much absent from home, and the training of his children devolved chiefly upon their mother, who taught them to read the Bible and to say their prayers morning and evening, and allowed them to run wild the rest of the time. Accordingly, Mary Fairfax spent a large portion of her time on the seashore, watching the birds and the shellfish, and admiring the seaweeds.

After a while she was sent to a boarding-school. Schools then were in great measure places of punishment, rather than of education; and especially was this true of those provided for girls. Mary was kept under severe restraint, "put in steel stays and busks and rods to improve her figure," and required to commit to memory page after page of Johnson's Dictionary. But though her school education was limited, she found means to improve herself; and, fortunately, she met with a friend in Dr. Somerville, of Jedburgh, who encouraged and aided her in her efforts to become a thorough scholar. Such encouragement was then doubly welcome; for it was considered "going out of the female province" for a woman to be a mathematician or a classical scholar. Miss Fairfax became an adept in Latin and Greek, as well as in mathematics; but she did not neglect those acquirements which are specially attractive in her sex, such as music and painting.

While still young, in her twenty-fourth year, she was married to Mr. Samuel Gray, Russian consul for Great Britain, and took up her abode in London. But her marriage did not put an end to her studies, for she soon undertook to obtain a knowledge of French, German, and Italian, that she might have access to scientific works in those languages.

Her married life lasted only three years, and on her husband's death she returned to her native land. Being left in independent circumstances, she was able to pursue any line of study she chose, however her friends might blame her for what they considered unwomanly conduct. Her uncle, Dr. Somerville, of whom we have already spoken, was in advance of his day in his views concerning the duties and privileges of women, and was ready at all times to defend her. In 1812 she was married to his son, a physician, and he, following the example of his father, entered with zeal into all his wife's studies, and from this time forth her life was a "happy round of scientific achievements."

Returning again to London, where her husband was professionally engaged, she pursued her studies, and in 1831 published her "Mechanism of the Heavens." This was followed in about two years by the work to which she owes her chief celebrity, "The Connection of the Physical Sciences," a work that won its way, notwithstanding the fact that its author was a woman, until it became a class-book at the universities. Honors came to Mrs. Somerville from foreign scientific societies, as well as from those at home, and a pension of two hundred pounds, afterwards increased to a larger amount, was granted her by the British government. To her earlier works she in course of time added others, such as "Physical Geography," and "Molecular and Microscopic Science."

Mrs. Somerville's health failing, she was compelled to seek a more genial clime, and she spent some time in Rome, Florence, Naples, and Geneva, with her husband and two daughters, who had now grown up to be their parents' companions and friends, as well as loved children.

Mrs. Somerville's great abilities and honors did not turn her thoughts away from her fellow-creatures and her God. She early espoused the anti-slavery and anti-press-gang causes, and in no measured terms denounced the cruelties of vivisection, though performed in the interests of science. Education for the poor, and a more liberal education for women, also found in her an able and zealous advocate.

Her daughter writes of her that when nearing the end of her journey "her mind was constantly occupied with thoughts of religion, and she lifted her heart yet more frequently to that good Father whom she had loved so fervently all her life, and in whose merciful care she fearlessly trusted in her last hour." To a friend who had sent her an essay on "Life After Death," she replied, "God bless you, dearest friend, for your irresistible arguments of our 'immortality;' not that I ever doubted it, but as I shall soon enter my ninety-third year, your words are an inexpressible comfort."

She took a special interest, even in her ninety-second year, and when only a short distance from the end of her journey on earth, in the discoveries of science.

One of her chief regrets was that she would "not see the distance of the earth from the sun determined by the observation of the transit of Venus, and learn the source of the most renowned of rivers, the discovery of which will immortalize the name of Dr. Livingstone." But while she did not live to obtain this information on earth, who can say that it is not already hers?

On the morning of November 29, 1872, she quietly fell asleep. Her daughters, watching by her bed, hardly knew the time of her passing away. But her noble example still lives. Let it stimulate others to attempt great things for Christ and humanity.

ANN HASSELTINE JUDSON.

NEAR the beginning of the present century there were two bright, happy girls attending the academy in Bradford, Massachusetts, Miss Atwood and Miss Hasseltine. They afterwards became celebrated for their devotion to the work of missions, at that early period when, even more than now, it involved untold sacrifices, and when it was not as fully appreciated by the church at large as it is at present. Nevertheless, at the call of duty, these young women bravely undertook the work, the one as Mrs. Newell, and the other as Mrs. Judson; and now their graves, in the Isle of France and in Burmah, tell of their sacrifice of life itself for the sake of the gospel.

Miss Hasseltine was born in Bradford, December 22, 1789. She was brought up in accordance with the forms of religion, and was largely controlled by its principles; yet for sixteen years she had no realizing sense of her sinfulness. Soon after she reached the age of sixteen, to use her own words, "the solemn truth that she must obtain a new heart or perish for ever impressed itself upon her mind," and she determined to secure peace and pardon; but how to find them she did not know. She tried self-imposed penances, and spent many weary hours trying to please God; but by this method she found no peace. At length, however, light broke into her mind: she saw Christ as the atoning Lamb of God, and was enabled to rejoice in the hope of salvation through his name. She was now in a new world, inspired by new hopes, and controlled by new motives, and she found great delight in the study of what some might regard as heavy theology. After leaving the Bradford academy, she engaged in teaching school, and manifested great interest in the spiritual, as well as the temporal, welfare of her pupils.

At the same period God's Spirit had been operating on the hearts of Messrs. Judson, Newell, Mills, Nott, and others, inclining them to seek the salvation of the heathen; and they laid their views of this matter before the General Congregational Association, which met at Bradford in 1810. At this meeting Miss Hasseltine made the acquaintance of Mr. Judson, and in the fall of the same year she received an offer of marriage from him. After careful and prayerful consideration of the question, she decided to cast in her lot with him in the arduous work of seeking the salvation of the people of India, for whose souls there were at that period few to care, while there were many to oppose sending them the gospel. No doubt she expected to meet with trials and sorrows in her work, but we have no idea that she imagined half the sufferings that she was to endure. And yet if she had realized them all, such was her consecration, such her pity for lost souls, that she would, no doubt, have braved all, and given her life willingly for Christ's cause and kingdom.

Mr. Judson did not picture to Miss Hasseltine a life of ease and comfort in their far-off home among the heathen. On the contrary, he wrote to her before their marriage, "If our lives are preserved, and our attempt prospered, we shall next New Year's Day be in India, and, perhaps, wish each other a happy New Year in the uncouth dialect of Hindostan or Burmah. We shall no more see our kind friends around us, or enjoy the conveniences of civilized life, or go to the house of God with those who keep holy day; but swarthy countenances will everywhere meet our eye, the jargon of an unknown tongue will assail our ears, and we shall witness the assemblies of the heathen to celebrate the worship of idol gods. We shall be weary of the world, and wish for wings like a dove, that we may fly away and be at rest. We shall probably experience seasons when we shall be 'exceeding sorrowful, even unto death.' We shall see many dreary, disconsolate hours, and feel a sinking of spirits, an anguish of mind, of which we now can form little conception. . . . . . But whether we shall be honored and mourned by strangers, God only knows. At least, either of us will be certain of one mourner. In view of such scenes shall we not pray with earnestness, 'Oh, for an overcoming faith,'?" etc.

But Miss Hasseltine's brave heart was not dismayed by even such possibilities. Accordingly, the marriage took place February 5, 1812, and on the next day Mr. Judson, with others, was ordained at Salem, Mass., as a missionary of the cross to India. In the same month, also, Mr. and Mrs. Judson sailed for India, arriving at Calcutta in June of the same year.

During the voyage they had occasion to examine the question of baptism, and changed their views in respect to it; but their work was too great, and their sacrifices too many, for them to be considered as merely denominational missionaries. Every denomination delights to refer to them as missionaries who have reflected honor on the church at large. They were welcomed to India by the venerable Dr. Carey, an English Baptist missionary, and found a home in the English mission-house at Serampore.

Soon, however, the American missionaries were ordered by the authorities under the East India Company to return to the United States. They were finally permitted to go to the Isle of France; and when they reached there, after many provoking delays, their friend Mr. Newell, who had arrived some weeks before, met them with the sad intelligence that his wife was now in her grave, instead of teaching the natives, as she had hoped, concerning the only Saviour. But though the Judsons sorrowed with their friend, they were not dismayed; they were confident that God was ordering all things wisely.

After some delay Mr. and Mrs. Judson found opportunity to sail for Rangoon in Burmah, where they arrived in July, 1813, and on June 27, 1819, their first convert was baptized. We can easily imagine the weary, patient, prayerful waiting of these missionaries to see the fruit of their labor. They sowed in tears, and by-and-by the reaping-time came. They waited long, but now thousands of converts are found in that once-benighted land. With the success of the mission, opposition to it was aroused, and Dr. Judson thought it wise to visit Ava, the residence of the king, to obtain from him protection. In this he failed, and had to commence his work anew, subject to increased annoyances.

The health of Mrs. Judson finally broke down amid her sufferings and labors, and she found it necessary to return to her native land. She arrived in New York in 1822, and by means of private and public letters did much to excite a missionary spirit among the churches. The following year, her health having been partially restored, she returned to India. Previous to this, however, the mission at Rangoon had been reinforced by Dr. Price, a medical missionary; and the fame of his cures had reached the palace at Ava. He was sent for, together with Dr. Judson, and persuaded to commence mission work in that city; and Dr. Judson removed there as soon as Mrs. Judson returned to Rangoon.

Very soon after the settlement of the missionaries in Ava, war was declared by the British against Burmah. Dr. Judson and others were arrested under the charge of being spies in the employ of the British government, and were thrust into the death-prison and loaded with chains. Mrs. Judson, also, was guarded in her own house by soldiers, so that for a few days she could do little to relieve the sufferings of her husband, or to save his life. She found means, however, of communicating with some of the officials, and, by a liberal use of money, secured some mitigation of her husband's sufferings in prison. She thus describes her labors for seven long months, during which she was every day uncertain what the result would be:

"The oppressions to which your brother and the other white prisoners were subject are indescribable. Sometimes sums of money were demanded, sometimes pieces of cloth and handkerchiefs; at other times an order would be issued that the white foreigners should not speak to each other, or have any communication with their friends without. Then, again, the servants were forbidden to carry in their food without an extra fee. Sometimes for days and days together I could not go into the prison till after dark, when I had two miles to walk in returning to the house. Oh, how many times have I returned from that dreary prison at nine o'clock at night, solitary and worn out with fatigue and anxiety, and thrown myself down in that same rocking-chair which you and Deacon L—— provided for me in Boston, and endeavored to invent some new scheme for the release of the prisoners."

At the end of this period Dr. Judson was removed, with other prisoners, to Oung-pon-la, where his treatment was even more severe; and if Mrs. Judson had not followed him, and with wonderful tact found means of helping him, he could not possibly have survived. Having found a home in a hut near the prison, she did much for the comfort of all the prisoners; but she was soon taken very sick, and lay at the point of death, unable to nurse her little babe; and had she not succeeded in bribing the jailer to allow Dr. Judson to leave the prison for an hour each day to carry poor little Maria around to nursing mothers, that she might suck a few drops of milk, the child would have died.

The end of this fearful suffering came, however, and Dr. Judson was released to act as interpreter between the Burmese and the British. Mrs. Judson then returned to Ava, but was prostrated with spotted fever, and narrowly escaped death. Providentially, Dr. Price was at the same time released from prison, and was able to supply her with the proper remedies, and thus she was again restored, but to find that Dr. Judson had again been committed to prison. She thus describes her feelings at that period:

"If ever I felt the value and efficiency of prayer, I did so at this time. I could not rise from my couch; I could make no efforts to secure my husband; I could only plead with that great and powerful Being who has said, 'Call upon me in the day of trouble, and I will hear, and thou shalt glorify me,' and who made me at this time feel so powerfully his promise that I became composed, feeling assured that my prayers would be answered."

And those prayers were answered; the same Holy Spirit who produced calmness and confidence in her mind, influenced the minds of the heathen around her, and Dr. Judson was saved. After the lapse of a few more days the missionary and his wife were guests of Sir Archibald Campbell, by whom reparation for lost property was obtained from the authorities of Ava; and, finally, after an absence of twenty-seven months, they reached the mission-house at Rangoon.

A new mission was commenced at Amherst, the capital of the territory ceded to England at the close of the war. Here Mrs. Judson was left with friends, while her husband accompanied the English envoy to Ava to arrange a commercial treaty, and secure, if possible, a clause favorable to mission work. But Dr. Judson was to see his wife's face no more. Before the negotiations were completed she was taken to the rest above, having been seized with a fever, from which, on account of her debilitated condition, resulting from her sufferings at Ava, she was unable to rally. Though her husband was absent, she was tenderly cared for, and so was her little Maria, who six months afterwards joined her mother in the spirit world.

Dr. Judson wrote to his sister in America, "Weep with me, my dear sister and parents, for my beloved wife is no more. She died at Amherst, October 24, 1826, of remittent fever, and is buried near the spot where she first landed. . . . . We will not mourn as those who have no hope, 'for if we believe that Jesus died and rose again, even so them also which sleep in Jesus will God bring with him.'"

Mrs. Judson was one of the noblest of women, one of the most heroic of missionaries. As the author of "The Earnest Man" well says, "She was one of the purest, brightest, sweetest spirits that ever gladdened home, and breathed into a husband's heart the sustaining, inspiring life of domestic love."

SARAH MARTIN.

In the parable of the talents the Saviour clearly teaches that he who has only one talent is under obligation to lay it out for God as certainly as if he had ten. Nor should any one permit himself to neglect this duty on the plea that the one talent can accomplish nothing. We have many examples where the one has accomplished far more than the five or the ten in other hands; and Sarah Martin's life furnishes just such an example, as will be seen by our sketch.

She was born at Caistor, in the County of Norfolk, England, in 1791. It was the period of the French Revolution; England was overrun with the atheistic doctrines of France, and little was done to elevate the masses of the people. The idea that Christian teaching could do more to maintain security for life and property than brute force had not yet been extensively adopted. But what could this child of poverty do to promote the acceptance of this important truth? We shall see.

She was the daughter of a shoemaker, but was early deprived by death of both her father and mother, and committed to the care of a widowed grandmother, equally poor with her parents as far as this world's wealth was concerned, but rich in faith, and an heir of the kingdom of heaven. Accordingly, she sought to impress upon Sarah's mind those precious truths which had been her own solace in the past, and were her hope for the future.

By the time that Sarah was twelve years of age, however, she manifested a decided aversion to the Bible; but, having a taste for reading, she devoted her time to other books, such as the Spectator, Shakespeare, and other English poets. Her mother's Bible she hid away, so that the sight of it should not reproach her. But one Sabbath morning, in the nineteenth year of her age, she, in pursuit of pleasure, left her home and walked to the neighboring town of Yarmouth, and, passing by a place of worship, out of mere curiosity entered. The sermon she heard was on the text (2 Cor. 5:11), "We persuade men," and strangely affected her. The hidden Bible was taken from its resting-place, and soon Sarah found "the light of the knowledge of the glory of God in the face of Jesus Christ."

Having experienced the blessedness of peace with God, the young dressmaker—for she had been working at that trade from her fourteenth year—now sought to tell others of her new joy.

She at once became a teacher in the Sunday-school, and began to visit the sick wards of the workhouse, where she became a ministering angel to many of the friendless ones in their dreary abode.

The Edinburgh "Review," speaking of the work done by Sarah Martin, thus describes the condition of the persons confined in Yarmouth jail: "The doors were simply locked upon the prisoners. Their time was given to swearing, gambling, playing, fighting, and bad language, and their visitors were admitted from without with little distinction. The whole place was filthy, confined, unhealthy, and its occupants were infected with vermin and skin diseases."

For years Sarah Martin desired to visit these poor prisoners, and read to them out of that book which she found so full of consolation to her own heart; but she could not muster up sufficient courage to make the attempt until the year 1819, in the twenty-eighth year of her age. Her first application was refused, but she persevered in her request, and at last was admitted, and permitted to read the twenty-third chapter of the Gospel of Luke to a woman imprisoned for cruelty to her child. The tears and thanks from that once hard heart encouraged Sarah to make further efforts, and as often as she could spare time from her daily labor she visited the gloomy prison, and read the Scriptures with its inmates.

She found most of the prisoners ignorant, and she began to teach them to read and write. But this could not be done efficiently in the few hours that she had hitherto taken from her daily labor; so she resolved to make the sacrifice of giving one whole day to this purpose, although it decreased her slender income one-sixth. Her method of teaching was simple. Those who did not know how to read she encouraged and aided in efforts to learn; and she induced those who could read to become teachers. The same plan was adopted in writing, and she supplied the prisoners with books, that they might copy and commit to memory extracts. She also persuaded them—and it needed some persuasion—to learn verses of Scripture, and repeat them to her on her weekly visits; and such was her success that she could write in her diary, "It astonishes me to observe how strictly and constantly the prisoners commit their verses from the Holy Scriptures every day. Poor old S—— takes uncommon pains to remember one every day. I——, who on April 21 could only attempt one, has for some time learned five regularly, and several of Watts' Divine Songs. Since yesterday he has learned fourteen from John 15 perfectly."

As far as the prisoners and the regulations of the prison were concerned, Sabbath and weekday were alike. There was no Sabbath service. It was literally true that no one, with the single exception of Sarah Martin, cared for the souls of these prisoners. She set to work to remedy this defect, and instituted a Sabbath service, which she conducted herself, as no one else was willing to take charge of it. A writer in the "Edinburgh Review" speaks of this service as follows: "The cold, labored eloquence which boy-bachelors are authorized, by custom and constituted authority, to inflict upon us . . . . sinks into utter worthlessness by the side of the jail addresses of this poor uneducated seamstress."

For three years she continued this ministry, and day by day earned her daily bread as seamstress, meditating, as she labored, what she could say and do to benefit the poor outcasts in whom she had become interested.

In addition to her religious work, she came to the conclusion that the prisoners must have something to do, to save them from the curse of idleness. Accordingly, with money which she solicited she purchased goods, cut them out in her home at night, and gave them to the women-prisoners to make, paying them so much for each garment, and then selling them. Finally, she formed a society called "The Female Prisoners' Employment Society," which accomplished much good, both morally and materially. She soon also found suitable employment for the men in making straw hats, bone spoons, etc.

Thus this poor dressmaker, with the motive power of love to Jesus in her heart, accomplished more for the reclamation of these prisoners than the so-called wise legislators, who from year to year were discussing the problem of what could be done to elevate and improve them.

Finally the magistrates of the city saw and acknowledged her good work, and voted to pay her the sum of twelve pounds, nearly sixty dollars, per annum. Not quite five dollars per month for her valuable services was what we should consider a miserable pittance, but it was of great value to her. At first she doubted whether she ought to accept it, lest it might be supposed that she was doing her work with a selfish motive, and thus prejudice might be created against it. Becoming convinced, however, that this pecuniary aid was providential, she gave herself wholly to the labor in which she delighted, and all her projects, including prison and workhouse instruction, an evening school for factory girls, and employment for discharged prisoners, were carried on under her skilful management and supervision.

And her work was not in vain. Many, profiting by her instruction, were reclaimed from vice and commenced a career of usefulness.

Evenings unclaimed by her factory girls, who met twice a week, were frequently spent among the sick in the workhouse or in the city; and, as her biographer writes, in the "Book of Noble English Women," "Many a dim eye lighted up with pleasure when she entered at the door; many a sore heart was strengthened by her soothing words of consolation and her accents of tenderness; many were the blessings showered upon her for gentle ministrations, for smoothed pillows and holy words of peace, for the sympathizing pressure of the hand and the sisterly kiss. Many a poor sufferer, in the isolation of the sick room, fancied he or she had entertained an angel unawares."

As in the case of Mrs. Fry, whose contemporary labors have already been sketched, it was not so much the work that Sarah Martin did personally—although that was certainly valuable, and all the more wonderful because of the circumstances under which it was done—as the fact that she became a teacher of others, and showed to philanthropists and legislators that even the most degraded could be reached and lifted up through the influences which Christianity supplies. There has been a great reformation in Great Britain respecting the treatment of prisoners, and Sarah Martin deserves to be held in lasting remembrance for her share of the work.

But the fifteenth of October, 1843, came at last, and with it the messenger of her Lord to call her to her rest. Her nurse told her that she believed her end was near. She replied, "Thank God! thank God!" and her spirit passed joyfully away.

In the light of this woman's life, who can dare hide her talents under the pretext that there is no opportunity to lay them out for God? If any one could use this argument, the poor orphan dressmaker of Yarmouth might; but she urged no such empty excuse. She did what she could, each effort enabling her to do more; and now her name is recorded on earth as a benefactress of many, and in heaven she doubtless rejoices in the presence of Him whom she loved and followed.

LADY HUNTINGDON.

At London, on the 17th of June, 1791, Lady Huntingdon, one of the most remarkable Christian women of any age, after whispering joyfully to her friends, "I shall go to my Father to-night," passed away, aged eighty-four years. Selina Shirley, afterwards Lady Huntingdon, was born near Ashby-de-la-Zouch, in Leicestershire, England, August 24, 1707; she was the second daughter of the Earl of Ferrers. The time of her birth and early years was a period of spiritual dearth and moral darkness, not only in England, but throughout her colonies. It was just before the Wesleys and Whitefield "lightened over England," and before the Tennents, Edwards, and others became instrumental in arousing spiritual life in our own country. The profession of religion seemed little more than a mere form; evangelical ministers were branded as fanatics, and it was popular to break up their meetings by mobs. As in apostolic times, such men were regarded as "turners of the world upside down," and especially were they frowned upon by the rich and the noble.

S. Huntingdon

But it was otherwise with the subject of our sketch. In the providence of God she was called in her early years to follow to the grave a beloved playmate, and when she saw the earth thrown on the coffin lid, and heard the mournful comment, "Earth to earth, ashes to ashes, dust to dust," her silent prayer was, "O God, be my God when my hour shall come."

That petition was prompted by the Holy Spirit, drawing her to her Heavenly Father; and although she had then no one near her to instruct her concerning "the Way, the Truth, and the Life," her serious impressions continued, and she afterwards found a teacher in her sister Margaret, who had been converted under the preaching of Mr. Ingham, whom she afterwards married.

At the age of twenty-one, Lady Selina was married to the Earl of Huntingdon, and became a model wife and mother; but for some time after her marriage she was ignorant of the blessings which flow from Christ. She then made the discovery that her formal observances, and the charities in which she abounded, could not wash away her sin and secure to her peace with God. She was laid upon a bed of sickness, and here new light beamed upon her soul. Like Paul, she was enabled to say, "God, who commanded the light to shine out of darkness, hath shined in our hearts, to give the light of the knowledge of the glory of God in the face of Jesus Christ;" and soon she consecrated herself in these words, "My God, I give myself to thee." Her sister Margaret's teaching, which she could not at first understand, was now plain to her: pardon and peace could be found only by unreserved trust in the Lord Jesus Christ our Saviour.

As soon as she was restored to health, she sent for John and Charles Wesley, who were then in London. These noble men, together with Whitefield, Ingham, and others, by their itinerant preaching, were arousing many from death-like slumbers to spiritual life and energy. They found in Lady Huntingdon a patron and friend, and her house in London became the meeting place for such men as we have named, and such as Watts, Doddridge, Col. Gardiner, and others.

Lady Huntingdon felt it to be her duty to call the attention of her friends to their need of an interest in the Lord Jesus Christ, a proceeding then altogether new, and she often met with a rebuff. The Duchess of Buckingham thus haughtily replied to one of her notes, "The doctrines of these preachers are most repulsive, and strongly tinctured with impertinence and disrespect towards their superiors, in perpetually endeavoring to level all ranks and to do away with all distinctions. It is monstrous to be told that you have a heart as sinful as the commonest wretches that crawl upon the earth. This is highly offensive and insulting, and I cannot but wonder that your ladyship should relish any sentiments so much at variance with high rank and good breeding."

Not only were Lady Huntingdon's efforts directed to the rich; she delighted to speak to the poor of the wondrous grace that is in Christ Jesus. The story has often been repeated of her conversation with a laborer in her garden, which was heard by another through a hole in the wall, and was the means of leading the unseen hearer to a knowledge of the Saviour. Thus did this noble woman labor to bring all with whom she came in contact to know and trust the Saviour so precious to her.

In 1746 her husband was suddenly taken away, and she was left to manage his wealth and to care for their children, a task to which she proved herself equal.

In January, 1739, Whitefield was announced to preach in Moorfields, then a common near London wall, where the rabble of the city were accustomed to assemble and hold daily and nightly revels. He was told that if he attempted to preach in such a place he would lose his life; but he made the attempt, and the result was, the great multitude was melted, and tears and groans issued from the most abandoned. He continued to preach there from a temporary shed, roughly thrown up, and called a tabernacle; but it was finally proposed to put up a more substantial building, which was finished and opened in June, 1753.

In November, 1756, another building was erected by Whitefield in the west end of London; it was known as Tottenham Court Chapel, and was, we believe, removed in 1830, being now used as a Congregational church.

About five years previous to the opening of the first building, Whitefield had been appointed chaplain to Lady Huntingdon, and preached frequently to many of the nobility in her mansion in Park street, London. While thus connected with her, he made several tours through the country, including Scotland. The leaders of the revived evangelical party were thus led into a correspondence with Lady Huntingdon, which resulted finally in the establishment of a college at Trevecca, Wales, where godly men could be trained for the ministry, and in the institution of numerous chapels all over the land, that the masses of the people might learn the way of salvation. So sadly was the evangelical doctrine obscured at that period by the formalism of the

Established Church, that a leading dignitary of the latter expressed his disapprobation of the earnestness of the new preachers, in a published sermon on "The great folly and danger of being righteous overmuch."

Lady Huntingdon, as a peeress of the realm, was able for a long time to give protection to her chaplains in their work of preaching the gospel, and she appointed for this purpose such men as Venn and Romaine; but by a decision of the courts, in 1779, the right of this protection was at last denied her, and the authority of the parish rector was declared paramount. Lady Huntingdon and a number of those pastors whom she specially aided were, therefore, under the necessity of taking advantage of the Toleration Act of 1689, which granted freedom of worship to dissenters from the Church of England, and seceding from the Established Church, with their congregations. Thus another denomination was added to the list in England, and known as the Countess of Huntingdon's Connection, though really consisting of Whitefield Methodists, the latter term having been first applied, in ridicule, to the Wesleys, Whitefield, and their associates, for their methodical habits of study and religious exercise while they were yet students in the university of Oxford. The Lady Huntingdon Connection differed from the Wesleyan Methodists in holding the Calvinistic doctrines of Whitefield; from the Independents in admitting the expediency of a scriptural liturgy; from the Church of England in their zeal to reach the masses with the gospel, and in their opposition to the legal formalities which prevented the free proclamation of the gospel without regard to parish lines.

The college at Trevecca was now a valuable auxiliary to the new denomination. The principal cause of the establishment of this college at the first, was the expulsion of several students from Oxford because they visited the hamlets of the poor, and tried to teach them the way of salvation. The charge against them was, "holding Methodistical tenets." On their expulsion, it was suggested that, as these six gentlemen were expelled for having too much religion, it would be very proper to inquire into the conduct of some who had too little. But at that period to be without religion was not regarded as a fault by many of the dignitaries of either the church or the nation. Soon the college furnished devoted ministers for the new denomination. In 1792 it was removed to Cheshunt, near London, where it still exists.

For over fifty years this noble woman used her influence, her time, and her wealth to promote the preaching of the gospel, and with wonderful success. She was styled in derision, by Horace Walpole, the queen of the Methodists, but it was certainly an honorable title, and probably no queen of England ever did so much work that would meet the approval of heaven as she did. But her work was finished at last. The infirmities of old age came upon her, rather than any special sickness; and after providing for her charities, and arranging for the carrying out of her plans, she went, as we have already described, to her Father's house in heaven.

LADY GLENORCHY.

"Not many mighty, not many noble, are called; but God hath chosen the foolish things of the world to confound the wise." But while there may not be many noble called to do the special work of the Lord on earth, there are a few, and among these we find the subject of our sketch—Lady Glenorchy. She was born at Preston, Scotland, in September, 1741, and was carefully educated under the superintendence of her mother, for her father, Dr. William Maxwell, died a few months before her birth. She early exhibited superior talents, especially in the line of music; and these endowments, together with her agreeable person and vivacious temperament, made her an object of admiration in the circles of fashion. She was married, in her twentieth year, to Lord Glenorchy, the only son of the Earl of Breadalbane, and with her husband she spent two years in France and Italy. On her return she became a votary of fashion, and indulged in the dissipations common to that period among the higher classes of society.

But soon the voice of God came to her in a

severe affliction; and, on her recovery, the Holy Spirit employed the truth contained in the first question of the Shorter Catechism of the Westminster Assembly to produce in her the conviction of her lost and ruined condition by reason of sin. This catechism she had been taught in early youth; and when she meditated on the fact that "the chief end of man is to glorify God, and to enjoy him for ever," she could not repress the inquiry, "Have I glorified God? Shall I enjoy him for ever?" Nor could she escape the conclusion that for more than twenty years she had been serving self and Satan, without any regard to the glory of God, or any desire to enjoy him hereafter.

At length, in her trouble, she wrote to a friend, Miss Hill, the sister of the Rev. Rowland Hill; and the answer that she received led her to search the Scriptures, with prayer that God would lead her to the truth. Soon afterwards, as she read part of the third chapter of Romans, the eyes of her spiritual understanding were opened, and that Saviour who had hitherto seemed to her "as a root out of a dry ground," without "form or comeliness," now appeared as "the chiefest among ten thousand," and "altogether lovely." From that period, four years after her marriage, to the end of her earthly journey, she and Miss

Hill were faithful friends and correspondents; and the latter, doubtless, did much to help her to withstand the temptations with which she was surrounded and the attempts to lead her back to the frivolities of fashionable life.

When Lady Glenorchy was in Edinburgh, where she spent a considerable portion of her time, she, with other distinguished ladies, formed a religious society, and met at each other's houses, and afterwards at the house of the minister of the High Church, Edinburgh, to study the Scriptures. It was in 1770 that she, with Lady Maxwell, conceived the design of opening a union church in Edinburgh, where ministers of all the evangelical churches might preach alternately. With this view St. Mary's Chapel was secured; but though large congregations assembled in it to hear the gospel, yet, in consequence of the opposition attending the enterprise, little was accomplished. The next effort of the kind was the building of a church in connection with the Established Church of Scotland; this church is, I believe, still known as Lady Glenorchy's Chapel.

In 1771 Lord Glenorchy died. He left to his wife the whole of his real and personal estate, and gave her power to use it "for encouraging the preaching of the gospel," etc. Nobly did she fulfil the trust committed to her care; and not only were her benefactions bestowed in Scotland, but also in England, where she had occasion, for the benefit of her health, frequently to sojourn. Indeed, so much was her heart in the work of the Lord, that she was not content to limit her expenditures for his cause to her annual income, but sold her estate at Barton, that she might use the proceeds in the upbuilding of her Master's kingdom. She acted on the principle laid down by Christ: "Lay up for yourselves treasures in heaven, where neither moth nor rust doth corrupt, and where thieves do not break through nor steal." If her example were only followed by half of the members of Christ's church, how soon, by the blessing of God, would the world be subdued to Christ.

Believing the circulation of tracts and books to be valuable as an instrumentality in promoting the Redeemer's kingdom, Lady Glenorchy gave her means in that direction; sometimes, indeed, she bore the whole expense of publishing a tract or book, that she might have it to circulate among her friends and the poor. Nor did she neglect the education of youth. Numerous teachers, in destitute localities, were employed and paid by her, that children might be trained for usefulness and in the fear of God. Indeed, she accomplished more by her single efforts and the expenditure of her own means, than some organized churches have been able to accomplish, though sustained by hundreds of members. Love to the divine Redeemer was the motive which prompted her actions; she could say, as did the apostle Paul, "The love of Christ constraineth me," and, as a consequence, her work was indeed a labor of love; she did not bestow her benefactions grudgingly, but in the spirit of Him who said, "It is more blessed to give than to receive."

But her work, carried on in her widowhood for fifteen years, reached its termination. On the fourteenth of July, 1786, she was seized with a disease which in three days released her from her labors below. She was at the house of the Countess of Sutherland, in Edinburgh, when the messenger came to her; and a relative, approaching her bed to find out whether she was asleep, heard her say, "Well, if this be dying, it is the pleasantest thing imaginable." From that time she slept peacefully, until she was taken home to the presence of that Saviour whom she had so ardently loved and so faithfully served. She was buried, agreeably to her own request, in a vault in the centre of the chapel in Edinburgh which she built in 1772.

MARY LYON.

AT South Hadley, Massachusetts, near the beautiful female seminary of Mt. Holyoke, known and loved by earnest workers in every quarter of the globe, stands a marble monument, with the following inscription on the west side:

MARY LYON,
The founder of
Mount Holyoke Female Seminary;
For twelve years its Principal,
and
A teacher for thirty-five years
and
Of more than three thousand pupils.
Born February 28, 1797,
Died March 5, 1849.

On the north side:

"Give her of the fruits of her hands; and let her own works praise her in the gates."

On the south side:

"Servant of God, well done!
Rest from thy loved employ;
The battle fought, the victory won,
Enter thy Master's joy."

On the east side, her own noble utterance in the last instruction she gave to her school:

"There is nothing in the universe that I fear but that I shall not know all my duty, or shall fail to do it."

To sketch the life and great work of her whose dust reposes under this monument is now our pleasant task. She was born, at the time already noted, in Buckland, near Ashfield, Mass., being the fifth of seven children. Both her parents were noted for their piety, and her mother was also said to have had more than usual force of mind. Her father died while Mary was in her fifth year. To her mother, therefore, she was chiefly indebted for early care and training; and well was Mrs. Lyon prepared for the task, and great was her reward—for all her children learned to love and serve their parents' God before they had passed the years of their youth.

It is supposed, from what Mary said to some of her early friends, that she was the subject of a change of heart in 1816, and that the instrumentality which the Holy Spirit employed was the simple explanation of Bible truth by her granduncle.

Soon after this she engaged in teaching school, receiving as compensation seventy-five cents per week, with board. To prepare herself better for this work she entered the Sanderson Academy, at

Ashfield, in the autumn of 1817. It was here her superior powers of mind were first manifested, and friends began to take a special interest in what they rightly judged to be a mind needing only a little polish to shine with uncommon brilliancy. The money that Miss Lyon had obtained from a brother, and by spinning, weaving, and teaching, was soon expended; but the trustees of the academy, to prevent her leaving, offered her the free use of its advantages. She then took all the housekeeping materials that she had gathered, in accordance with the common practice of young women at that time, and exchanged them at a boarding-house for board.

Being thus prepared for teaching, she found no difficulty in finding employment; and when she had gathered more money by her work, in 1821 she entered, in pursuit of still higher qualifications, Rev. Joseph Emerson's school, at Byfield, near Newburyport, Mass. It was while attending this school that her religious character was more fully developed, and that she obtained boldness to witness for Christ. Her pen, too, found a new subject for correspondence. Writing to her mother at this period, she said that Miss Grant, with whom she afterwards was associated at Ipswich, had expressed her views in a most affecting manner. "She feared," wrote Miss

Lyon, "that the Saviour was here wounded in the house of his friends; that Christians in this school were grieving the Holy Spirit; that the state of their hearts presented obstacles to his special presence and work. The solemnity, affection, and tender solicitude with which she uttered these remarks appeared to make a deep impression on every mind. Since that a visible change has been in progress in the school. Sometimes during devotional exercises, or while listening to Mr. Emerson's instructions and solemn warnings, scarcely a heart has been able to refrain from sighs, or an eye from tears." In an atmosphere like this Miss Lyon made rapid progress in the divine life, as well as in secular knowledge.

Soon after this Miss Lyon engaged to teach in the academy which she herself had first attended at Ashfield, where she continued until persuaded by Miss Grant to join her as associate principal in a school at Londonderry, N. H. Partly on account of the severity of the climate, this school was not held in winter; hence Miss Lyon taught, at the same time, a winter school at Buckland; and when Miss Grant moved her school to Ipswich, Mass., Miss Lyon accompanied her, but still continued her independent school.

God abundantly blessed her labors, and gave

her warm friends. He was preparing her and those who were to be her helpers for the great work that she was by-and-by to perform at South Hadley. But Miss Lyon's work during these years was itself of great importance. She sent out numerous teachers from her schools, imbued with her unselfish spirit; and wherever they went they created an enthusiasm in behalf of education and religion, so that to have been a pupil of Miss Lyon's was considered the very best recommendation for a teacher.

From 1831 to 1834 she gave her whole time to the Ipswich school. While there, she meditated on the establishment of such a school as Mt. Holyoke, until the thought became, to use her own words, "as fire in her bones." She felt that many noble minds were left, to use the figure of Gray, to "waste their sweetness on the desert air," because of the expense attending the obtaining of an education. This obstacle she determined to overcome, and finally accomplished her purpose by establishing the seminary at Mt. Holyoke, where an education could be obtained at a rate much below what was charged at similar institutions.

But she had undertaken a difficult task. The value of female education was not then appreciated as it is at the present time. The country was comparatively poor; men were not in the habit of giving large sums for any purpose, and it was a very easy matter to find an excuse for not contributing to what was then only an experiment. Miss Lyon, however, met and surmounted all these difficulties. Her first work was to disseminate information by means of a well-prepared circular, which she followed up by personal application. She had well considered the difficulty of the undertaking, but she had strong faith in the God of providence. A little before she said farewell to her friends at Ipswich, she wrote to a sister as follows: "I never had a prospect of engaging in any labor which seemed so directly the work of the Lord as this. It is very sweet, in the midst of darkness and doubt, to commit the whole to his guidance."

Her trust was not disappointed. She was about to experience the truth of the Psalmist's declaration, "Commit thy way unto the Lord: trust also in him: and he shall bring it to pass." On September 6, 1834, a few friends, whom Miss Lyon had enlisted by correspondence, met in her parlor, and appointed a committee to take steps to raise funds, etc. Miss Lyon herself went to work, and collected from her lady friends one thousand dollars to meet the outlay of carrying on the project. After a while the question of location was settled, and Rev. Roswell Hawks was engaged to collect funds for the erection of buildings. With the aid of Miss Lyon, who often accompanied him in his work, some progress was made, and the cornerstone of the building was laid October 3, 1836. In the meantime, Miss Lyon had enlisted, or, rather, as she herself believed, the Holy Spirit had inclined to her project, the hearts of such men as Joseph Avery, of Conway, Deacon A. W. Porter, of Munson, and Deacons Safford and Williston; and in such hands there was no danger of failure.

Accordingly, the school, whose fame afterwards not only spread through our own land, for its noble work of Christian education and the teachers it has supplied in almost every part of our country, but which became celebrated in nearly every portion of the world for the missionaries it has educated and sent out, and which, we doubt not, is also noted in heaven as the place where many have been born into the kingdom of our Lord and Saviour Jesus Christ, was opened November 8, 1837, a little over three years after the meeting in Miss Lyon's parlor at Ipswich. There were rooms for eighty pupils, and such was the reputation of Miss Lyon that more than could be accommodated made application within a few days. What wonderful things God had wrought for her! Well might her biographer say, "She had long been one of those who, observing providences, have providences to observe."

The peculiarities of the seminary are so well known that we need only name them. First, there were no day scholars; all the pupils were required to room and board within its walls. Secondly, to lessen expense, and bring the cost of education to rates that the middle classes could afford, and to educate the young women in domestic matters, all the work in the building was to be performed by the teachers and pupils. And, thirdly, direct and persistent efforts were to be put forth for the salvation of the souls of the pupils. Wonderful was the success which the school attained in all these respects. There were few years, indeed, during Miss Lyon's life when it was not visited with the special influences of the Holy Spirit, so that in Miss Lyon's latter years, when speaking of the death of loved ones who had studied within its walls, she could say, "I thank God that I have not yet heard of the death of any pupil of this beloved seminary who was without a hope in Jesus."

But her twelve years of busy labor soon came to an end. In February, 1849, a pupil died of erysipelas. As she lay at the point of death, the whole school was touched and solemnized. Miss

Lyon, who at the time was not in her usual health, was specially moved, and, feeble as she was, desired to use the condition of the loved one for the spiritual profit of the whole school. She accordingly met with the students in the hall, and, in the words of one who was present, "she wished to lead us to turn from the trying circumstances in which we were placed and follow that dear dying one up to the 'celestial city,' and, as its pearly gates opened to receive her, look in and catch a glimpse of its glories. She seemed to have a most enrapturing view of heaven, and with a full heart exclaimed, 'Oh, if it were I, how happy I should be to go,' but added, 'Not that I would be unclothed while I can do anything for you, my dear children.'"

It was in this address that she uttered the noble sentiment which is inscribed on her tombstone.

The time when she, too, should hear the welcome voice, "Come up higher," was only a few days further off. The same disease that had taken her pupil called her away; but it was to a Saviour she loved, and to a heaven she longed for; and now, in the grounds of the seminary, the offspring of her special labor and prayers, her body awaits the resurrection of the just.

In an address at the first anniversary of the

seminary after her death, among other things Dr. Hitchcock said of her: "From the days of her childhood to the time of her death, all her physical, intellectual, and moral powers were concentrated upon some useful and noble object, while selfishness and self-gratification seem never to have stood at all in the way, or to have retarded the fervent wheels of benevolence. I cannot, therefore, believe that it is the partiality of personal friendship which leads me to place Miss Lyon among the most remarkable woman of her generation. Her history, too, shows the guiding hand of special providence almost as strikingly as the miraculous history of Abraham, of Moses, of Elijah, or of Paul. Oh, it tells us how blessed it is to trust Providence implicitly when we are trying to do good, though the darkness be so thick around us that we cannot see forward one hand's breadth, and bids us advance with as confident a step as if all were light before us."

Well would it be for every land to have many such noble women.

www.ingramcontent.com/pod-product-compliance
Lightning Source LLC
Chambersburg PA
CBHW020312240426
43673CB00039B/786